RadioActiveTimes

Based on the BBC Radio 4 series 'Radio Active'
by Angus Deayton and Geoffrey Perkins
Winners of BPI Award for Best Radio Comedy
Show 1981, Sony Award for Best Light
Entertainment Programme 1982, and the
Premio Ondas 1983

First published in Great Britain
by Sphere Books Ltd 1986
27 Wrights Lane, London W8 5TZ

Produced by Adamson Books

Copyright © 1986
Angus Deayton & Geoffrey Perkins

Authors	Angus Deayton
	Geoffrey Perkins
Anna Daptor	Helen Atkinson-Wood
Martin Brown	Michael Fenton Stevens
Mike Channel	Angus Deayton
Mike Flex	Geoffrey Perkins
Nigel Pry	Philip Pope

Contents

Sir Norman Tonsil

The Chairman of Radio Active looks back over last week's achievements

THE WEEK has been a good one. Seven solid days with 24 hours in each.

Would that the same could be said of this week's output on Radio Active... Last week began with a genuine attempt on our part to cater for minority audiences. Our Sunday morning programme for the Indian community entitled *Hello Indians* was followed by another early morning show, fronted by our Asian and African friends, which we called *Breakfast with the Bimbos*. Although it was at my instigation, the IBA were less than enthusiastic and sued. Many also saw this as the most likely reason behind the race riot at Radio Active's Fun Day last Tuesday.

Then there was our religious adviser's dramatic attack of flatulence during the *Epilogue*, the 45-minute speech by the Prime Minister which we broadcast backwards (although no-one seemed to notice), the arrest of our cookery expert for offences relating to the disappearance of over 200 assorted household pets, and the incident with the sheep during the hobbies programme.

Let us hope the coming week brings more success and fewer writs. I, for my part, will be spending much of it with a brandy and cigar in my office, sitting next to the radio – just in case anyone has the smart idea of trying to turn it on. ∎

Sir Norman: 'More success and fewer writs'

Sir Norman Tonsil hosts 'Did You Catch It?' – a review of the week's broadcasting, every Tuesday afternoon at 4.30pm (see Saturday, 10.0pm).

Radio Active's Centenary — Nineteen Years Old

A brief history of the station to mark Radio Active's nineteenth birthday, as told by some of its star DJs

Yes, Tuesday marks the big one. Nineteen years ago, almost exactly, Radio Active first started broadcasting as a pirate radio station from an old weather ship in the North Sea. And one man still occasionally heard on the station today was on the air right from the outset. The Grand Old Man of the airwaves – **Mike Channel.**

Mike Channel in 1968

'Yes, I was one of the pioneers, one of the people who made the way easy for some of the other DJs who were to come along later and jump on the bandwagon. As one of the first DJs it fell to me to recruit

Radio Active's Nineteenth Birthday Wednesday all day

other jocks, and I regret to say that I was responsible for suggesting Nigel Pry, Mike Flex and Uncle Mike Stand, who was keen to join a ship outside government jurisdiction at very short notice.'

One of the most popular records at the time was the Beatles' White album which received more airplay than any other record on the station. This was because it was the only record owned by the station, and for five months it was the only thing we broadcast apart from the occasional MayDay signals. But several guests were persuaded to drop in on the ship, amongst them **Mick Jagger.**

Mick Jagger

'Yes, I remember the ship very well,' Mick Jagger confesses. 'For instance, do you know that the ship had 12 life belts, 16 steps between kitchen and the main deck, and a total of 37 door handles? I know all about this because I was stuck on it for three months. In fact it was during that period that I first considered retiring, because I figured that by the time I finally got off the ship not too many of my fans were going to remember who I was.

But you know, I've often thought about the ship, and I really think that if someone else hadn't beaten me to it, I would have liked to come back with a couple of jets and sunk it.'

Nigel Pry

The man who beat Mick to it was the young Nigel Pry who succeeded during a demonstration of how to make banana flambé in flambéing the station into the bargain. Several of the early jocks remember the sad day when they looked back on the burning hulk, going down in a holocaust of rum and raisin,

a day made all the sadder by the fact that Nigel managed to climb into the lifeboat with everyone else.

And so Radio Active came ashore, where they caught the attention of a leading businessman, a man of boldness and vision, a man who commissioned this article, Sir **Norman Tonsil**, the man whose braille version of the *Sun* was enjoying considerable success, particularly page 3. He told our reporter how the vision of the benefits of commercial radio came to him. **Sir Norman:**

'I remember I was driving along one day in one of my Rolls when radio came dramatically into my life in the form of a young man who suddenly crashed through my window carrying one. Apparently he had been holding it to his ear as he crossed the road, and so engrossed was he in the sounds coming out of it that he failed to see me jump the lights. I saw him in good time but I was unable to stop because I have never seen the necessity of having brakes installed in my car. Well, I was immediately struck by the power of radio when it caught me a nasty thwack on the ear as he flew past me and out of the rear window, and somewhat later I became aware of its potential financial rewards when I successfully sued the young man in question for substantial damages. I'm glad to say that this is one country where the word of a rich businessman will always be believed against that of a yob.

Later my accountant was to alert me to the possible benefits of owning my own station, particularly in the artistically creative field of 'Tax losses'. As to why it should have been Radio Active, that is a question I have been asking myself ever since.'

This was the site Sir Norman chose for the new station

Within two years he had transformed it into this

It opened in 1972, with a gala showbiz party featuring many of the top celebrities of the time. People like the 1970 Midland Area Foxtrot runners up from *Come Dancing;* the woman who appeared in John Alderton's sit com., *My Wife Next Door* as his wife next door's next door neighbour's wife; the Austrian who came seventh in the 1968 Eurovision Song contest; the man who left his sponge bag behind in his room in Episode 865 of *Crossroads;* the woman who played all those fat, blonde tarty bar maids in some of the lesser known fifties British B movies; the man who provided the knees for Jonathan Miller's *The Body in Question;* the Invisible Man's stand-in from the 1958 TV series; a ball of string that appeared regularly in the puppet show *Fireball XL5;* and Simon Dee.

Since then, of course, many more famous faces, and several famous pairs of legs, have climbed the equally famous Radio Active staircase, and then climbed down again when they have discovered that it is not actually connected to the first floor.

But certainly few of the DJ's who were there for the grand opening could have guessed that in under fifteen years' time the station would have gone from having just two studios and a reception area to having one studio and a broom cupboard.

Not all the jocks who started with us then are still with us. One of those who has gone on to other things is Dick Jones, who left us in 1978 to make way for the up and coming Mike Flex.

Dick Jones:

❛ Well, I'm very happy now, doing 'my own thing' as they say. I have my own toilet to look after, Monday to Friday, and somebody else comes in on weekends. And when I'm not there I leave it all behind. I'm not one of those people who take their work home with them. But I don't think I miss the glamour of being a disc jockey, or the fame… or the pots of money… or the fast cars and glamorous women. No, I'd choose working 9 to 5 in a toilet any day.

Of course, I'd be lying if I didn't say I felt *tinges* of bitterness towards Mike Flex, and I must admit I have made one or two attempts on his life. But that hatred's all gone, and if I met him in the street now I'd shake him by the hand. 'Course, if he came in my toilet I'd chop his willy off. ❜

So what of the next nineteen years? **Mike Channel:**

❛ Well, if I'm not sharing a mop with Dick Jones I shall probably still be around, giving the occasional Ark Ark as Aaron the Aadvark on *Wey, Hey, It's Saturday* whenever I'm asked. ❜

Mike Flex:

❛ Well, maybe I'll be popping back to host the odd peak time show, but I expect I'll be on telly most of the time by then, and Mike Channel will be on the heart and lung machine. ❜

Dick Jones

RADIO ACTIVE EDITOR

Probe Round The Back Thursday 11am

This week's Probe Round The Back takes a look at one of the station's oldest employees, the editor, Malcolm Watts, whose job it is to edit down bits of speech and dialogue without altering the sense of them too much.

A LOOK at the unedited version of a speech made by a Labour spokesman on immigration shows how editing can help. Malcolm Watts judiciously edited out the redundant words, shown in italics.

'Firstly, I am personally *convinced that this government's immigration policy is* crass and retarded. And anything *they do,* I say *now,* should be subject to the utmost scepticism and, hopefully, ignored. For example, in reality, I am *sure the rights of* a black *man and* woman with a large family *are not properly guarded.* I am *driven mad by politicians* and *the like who believe such people* should be simply regarded as a *family of* social outcasts and deported at the earliest opportunity. Get rid of *racism, and believe* me, the world will be a better place.' ∎

FACT FILES

Listeners often write in to ask for personal details of our DJs. Here are profiles of the people who have helped to make Radio Active what it is today

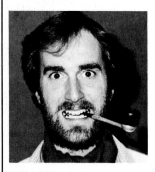

Mike Channel

BIRTHDATE: 6th January 1946
BIRTHPLACE: St Thomas Hospital, London
SCHOOLS: Marlborough Public School
A & O LEVELS: None
FAVOURITE FOOD: Sweetbreads in aspic
FAVOURITE DRINK: Real Ale (Bullocks Old Scrumptious if they have it)
FAVOURITE ARTIST: Barry Manilow and Aled Jones
HOBBIES: Cricket and trivial pursuit (sometimes the same thing!)
CAREER DETAILS: British Forces Broadcasting Service 1966. BBC Radio Newscaster 1967. Peak-time mid-morning show on Radio Active 1967-85. Weekend show at 4am on Sundays 1985-6. Aaron the Aardvark in Saturday morning kiddies show, ATP
SIR NORMAN TONSIL'S COMMENT: A prize Noddy, if ever I saw one

Mike Flex

BIRTHDATE: 6th January 1959
BIRTHPLACE: Room 413, Holiday Inn, Miami, Florida
SCHOOLS: St John's Enfield, Oakhurst Grammar, Beechwood Grammar, Cambridge Tutors, Weybridge 6th Form College, Harwood 6th Form College, Bridge House 6th Form College, Cambridge Tutors, Lastditch Crammer
A & O LEVELS: None
FAVOURITE FOOD: Big Mac
FAVOURITE DRINK: Coke
FAVOURITE ARTIST: Ozzy Osbourne and Alice Cooper
HOBBIES: American Football and Custom Cars
CAREER DETAILS: Joined Radio Active at 19. Worked on Mike Channel Show as tea-boy, weatherman, newscaster, co-host and finally presenter, following Mike Channel's move to his new popular weekend slot
SIR NORMAN TONSIL'S COMMENT: A cocky, off-the-wrist sort of toss-pot

Anna Daptor

BIRTHDATE: 14 March 19~~68~~
BIRTHPLACE: Hospital bed
SCHOOLS: St Anne's Convent, Cheltenham
A & O LEVELS: Art (0)
FAVOURITE FOOD: Lunch
FAVOURITE DRINK: Natural additive-free fruit juices and Polish vodka
FAVOURITE ARTIST: Julio Iglesias
HOBBIES: See Favourite Food
CAREER DETAILS: BBC Radio Dogger Bank 1969-79, Radio Active Lunchtime Show 1979-86. Also presenter of The Food Show (1984), The Joy of Eating (1985), Food and More Food (1985), and Dieting for Fatsos (1986)
SIR NORMAN TONSIL'S COMMENT: A fat head with a backside to match

Martin Brown

BIRTHDATE: 13th to 19th August 1959
BIRTHPLACE: Between 3rd and 4th Floors of British Home Stores
SCHOOLS: None
A & O LEVELS: None
FAVOURITE FOOD: Smarties
FAVOURITE DRINK: Orange Squash
FAVOURITE ARTIST: Enid Blyton

HOBBIES: Collecting badge to stick on anorak
CAREER DETAILS: Quee~~n~~ Elizabeth Hospital Radi~~o~~ 1980-84. Radio Activ~~e~~ January 1985. Queen Eliza~~-~~ beth Hospital Radio Februar~~y~~ 1985-September 1986. Radi~~o~~ Active 'Out Of Your Depth~~'~~ programme September 1986~~-~~ Radio Pentonville ATP
SIR NORMAN TONSIL'~~S~~ COMMENT: An imbecile. ~~A~~ man barely housetrained~~.~~ Cheap, however

Nigel Pry

BIRTHDATE: Unknown
BIRTHPLACE: Unknown
SCHOOLS: St Cuthbert~~'s~~ Reform, Forest Hill Remand~~,~~ St Lawrence's psychiatri~~c~~ wing day school, Wormwoo~~d~~ Scrubbs Comprehensive, S~~t~~ Theresa's Borstal
A & O LEVELS: Use o~~f~~ English (A)
FAVOURITE FOOD: Roas~~t~~ Beef with Custard
FAVOURITE DRINK: Alcoho~~l~~
FAVOURITE ARTIST: Pardo~~n~~
FAVOURITE ARTIST: Yes
HOBBIES: What?
CAREER DETAILS: Eh?
CAREER DETAILS: N~~o~~ thank you
SIR NORMAN TONSIL'~~S~~ COMMENT: A complete cab~~-~~ bage head

NOW AT LAST

THERE'S A

NEW DRINK

HAT'S TRULY

EXCITING

IT'S THE

TASTE THAT

PUTS THE

BLEEEUGHH

IN FEELSIQUE*

FEELSIQUE

A Subtle Blend of Tomato Juice and Whisky From 'HONEST' RON

FEELSIQUE is a trademark of 'Honest' Ron Bacardi & Co. Ltd

98% Vol e 71cl

*KEEP IT DOWN AND WIN A MINI METRO

WHAT DID I EVER DO?

A brand new quiz game in which each week a panel of 'celebrities' appear and members of the public have to guess what the hell it was they did to make them famous

Thursday 11.0

WE CAN certainly promise you a few surprises in the course of this new series. For instance, did you know:

Lionel Blair

did *not* compose *Oliver!*, as several people thought. In fact he was the man behind the Lionel Blair Dancers, of household fame themselves, of course.

Robert Dougall

the man we now know from the Reader's Digest give away offer ads, was actually a newsreader. Quite rightly he became famous for the difficult job of reading out pieces of paper that people gave him.

Leslie Crowther

proved to be a real puzzler for our panel. Sandra Kingsley of Kenton came closest with 'He's no bloody good at anything', but in fact the correct answer was that he was an 'All-Round Family Entertainer', perhaps best known for giving away pencils on *Crackerjack*. That was in his younger days before his hair turned black.

Victoria Principal

was another one to stump our audience. Although most people guessed what she was famous for, it came as a surprise to discover that she has in fact never done it professionally.

Arianna Stassinopoulos

the celebrated Greek something or other, was of course originally famous for having been bonked by the diminutive man of letters Bernard Levin, although some people thought he must have been put up to it.

Steve Race

the sometimes bearded presenter of the popular show *My Mistake, I Thought This Programme Was Supposed to Be Entertaining*, did indeed, as one member of the audience pointed out, once write a song which got to number 87 in Iceland, and which is constantly being heard on the radio on programmes hosted by Steve Race, but in fact his main claim to fame is that he can grow a beard if required.

The audience were also flummoxed when asked to name the shows that various 'top actors' had acted in. In fact neither **Joanna Lumley** nor **Gareth Hunt** have ever actually acted in anything, although they did both appear in a show called *The New Avengers*.

And finally **Gyles Brandreth** was in fact a trick question. He turned out not to be a celebrity at all!

So lots of fun in store at eleven o'clock this Thursday when you can join David Vine, Katie Boyle and Aneka Rice and hear them ask the question, 'What Did I Ever Do?' ■

Sister Ellen: from another era

Nun So Fair

This week Mike Channel meets another very 'Special Person'

Special Person Thursday 11.0

SISTER ELLEN is 94 years old. And she's been in the convent of St Theresa of the Witterings for almost eighty of them. When she entered the convent Queen Victoria had just died, man had yet to fly, the internal combustion engine had only just been invented and beer was a penny a pint.

The twentieth century has, as it were, passed her completely by. She hasn't even been in a car. So what, in all her time has she missed most? What is the one thing she would, perhaps, have liked to have had? She thought long and hard about my question, and then looking up at me with those dreamy, heavy lidded eyes that seemed to come from another era, she said, 'A digital watch. And a Sony Beetamax Portable Video Cassette recorder. And a ra-ra skirt.' And as soon as she had spoken she sank back to contemplate that long gone world of eighty years ago which was the only world she knew outside the convent.

I asked her if it was true that she had never been in a car. She said, yes, it was true. Because she had her own 850cc Harley Davidson. Would I like a ride on it? I told her, no, it was alright, I'd take a taxi back to the station. She gave me a card with the number of a mini-cab firm in Isleworth and told me that she'd always found them very reliable. And so I left her, staring wistfully out of the ancient stained glass window of the convent, no doubt remembering those long lost Edwardian summers, as she nibbled reflectively on her Big Mac and French fries. ■

SLEAK ALUMINIUM FINISH

0–60 IN UNDER 10 SECONDS

CRUISES COMFORTABLY AT 90 MPH

6000cc TWIN-TURBO ENGINE

TWIN OVERHEAD CAMSHAFTS

FUEL-INJECTED MOTOR

AUTOMATIC TRANSMISSION AND ELECTRONIC RELAY

PANORAMIC ROOF GARDENS

HEATED PLUNGE POOL

GENUINE SCANDINAVIAN SAUNA

<u>AND</u> YOU CAN HAVE SEX WITH IT

THE NEW TRIUMPH VONGOLE

— ONE HELLUVA BIKE

Another Thodding By-Election

This Thursday Radio Active will be reporting from the all-important Thodding By-Election, where our chairman Sir Norman Tonsil is himself standing as a candidate for the Free-Enterprise-Bring-Back-the-Rack-and-Send-Home-All-Those-With-a-Touch-of-the-Tarbrush-in-Them Democratic Party

By-Election Special
Thursday 11.0

THODDING has seen many changes. Twenty years ago there were fields all around the outskirts of the town. Today there are factories on the outskirts, while the centre of the town is all fields. The by-election has been caused by the disappearance of its last MP, John Stonewall, who vanished after embezzling the contents of a guide dog for the blind, and his clothes were found on a beach in Devon. Later, of course, he turned up in Australia, where he was arrested for wandering around Melbourne with nothing on.

Sir Norman Tonsil says: I decided to stand in the Thodding By-Election as an Independent because I felt that the policies of the Conservative party are far too left wing. Over the last few weeks I have endeavoured to meet as many of the constituents as possible. I've even spoken to some working class people, some of whom were actually quite rational with two arms, two legs and a head. And that impressed me. In addition I have been sympathising with local workers, making promises to local housewives, and buying large gifts for local businessmen.

Sir Norman's Manifesto

Sir Norman campaigns for the younger vote

JASMINE COTTAGE, CROWSLEY, OXON

Let me say my first priority will be to get the unemployment figures down. No one likes seeing them displayed in public, and I shall therefore be taking them down as soon as I am elected.

Secondly, I am not, as is being rumoured, in favour of amassing a huge arsenal of nuclear weapons. I am in fact all for getting rid of them. Half of them over Moscow, and the rest over the Arab chappies. Pensions and housing are also high up on my list, as I'm looking to take out two or three new pensions and buy a considerable number of new houses if I am elected.

Finally, I would like to dismiss the notion that I have simply stood in this by-election as a publicity stunt. Though, this charge may be true of the SDP. And of the Little Cottage Restaurant, Open 12.30 to 2.30, 7.30 to 11.00. Must Book Fridays and Saturdays Not Open On Sundays Party.

Radio Active will be providing complete coverage of the election, with the help of our computer colour graph, which should prove, if our predictions are correct, a complete waste of money on radio.

And following the first findings of our straw poll when a Mrs Eileen Simpkin said she intended to vote Conservative the computer has declared that if that trend is reflected in the rest of the constituency it would mean a landslide victory for the Tories with none of the other parties getting any votes at all. And on a national scale, a majority for the Conservative

David Whittle, SDP

POST CARD

Dear Voters,

As someone who lives outside the constituency I feel I can, perhaps, take a broader view of Thodding than many of the other candidates. Living as I do in the Seychelles I think I can put the problems of Thodding into the wider context of the Indian Ocean. And indeed already I have found that there are several Thoddings – there's one in Yorkshire, and there's one in the Isle of Wight, which is where I am at the moment. Hope to be with you in time for the actual count.

Best wishes, David.

P.S. weather is lovely. Wish you were here.

The picturesque town

Thodding has seen many changes. Today it's a bustling market town in the middle of Gloucestershire; but only a few years ago it was a sleepy harbour in Cornwall

The Fringe Party Manifestos

Militant NOT

Ray Yardley, Labour

Firstly let me deny that I am, or have ever been, a member of Militant. I say this because

1. I don't want to be thrown out of the Labour Party
2. They wouldn't let me join.

My policies place me, I believe, firmly in the mainstream of the Labour party.

They are:

● The immediate execution of the Royal family.
● Nationalisation of all local shrubs.
● The abolition of the colour blue.
● A closed shop agreement whereby all the shops in Thodding will be closed and replaced by one enormous government-run store which will sell only potatoes.

Conservative Party

Christopher Whitfield, Conservative

Firstly, let me say that I am not the sort of politician who makes promises that he cannot keep. So you can believe me when I promise to reduce rates, reduce taxes and increase government expenditure on local amenities. I will make sure that any essential repair work you might need doing to your houses is done immediately.

In addition I promise all the electorate that I will personally do little odd jobs around the place for you. I will undertake to do your washing up, take the dog down the park and prepare all your evening meals. So if you're fed up with other politicians' empty promises vote for Christopher Whitfield, and make sure that your laundry comes up really clean.

Chris. Whitfield

party at the next General Election of some 650 seats to none, which if we project this into the future, would last forever. This would mean that unemployment would continue to rise at the current rate, leading to massive inner

city unrest, with a probable workers' revolution which would inevitably drag in the super powers leading to all out nuclear war and the devastation of all life on earth.

So that's what we're

expecting. And in addition we'll be talking to some of the entertainers who have turned up in Thodding. Billy Connolly has turned out for Labour, John Cleese has turned out for the SDP, while, unfortunately, Sir

Norman Tonsil has been badly harmed by receiving support from Gyles Brandreth (see 'What Did I Ever Do?' Thursday 11am, feature p.12)

A RIGHT REPUTABLE REP!

What week would be complete without an offering from Radio Active's Repertory Company? Sadly none, and this week we feature the little-known faces behind the lesser-known voices

Die Muttervölker von Köln
Tuesday 1am

JEREMY BOTTOMS is often regarded as the Grand Old Man of the Drama Rep., though his white handlebar moustache and his perennial Edwardian smoking jacket, walking stick and snuff box can sometimes mislead people who fail to realise that he is, in reality, 27.

In fact Frederick Dodd is the real Grand Old Man, being the only surviving member of the original rep. which was founded fifteen years ago. He did subsequently leave to pursue his theatrical ambitions, twice understudying Tony Brandon as Buttons at Worthing Repertory Theatre, before spending a glittering five years as a cavity wall insulator until the firm went into liquidation and he sadly rejoined the Rep.

Jacques Rennard has delighted over the years since he joined us from the Massif Central School of Speech and Artistic Temperament in Paris. As Molière's Tartuffe, one critic said, he 'truly gave the play an authentically French atmosphere'. His Hamlet led another to call him 'A truly French prince. You could almost smell the Seine running through the Danish court,' while of his Thomas Hardy's West Country rustic Gabriel Oak in *Far From the Madding Crowd* another wrote: 'You could practically hear him swinging on the bells of Notre Dame.' When asked whether his complete inability to speak the English language was any sort of hindrance to him he replied 'Non, il ne faut pas détruire les écureils.'

Dame Claire Bunting admits that Dame is an unusual Christian name, but in fact she comes from a distinguished theatrical family. Her mother was part of Donald Wolfitt's company, where she had the distinction of appearing on stage opposite the great man when she fell off her prompt stool. She herself remembers playing in twice-weekly rep., where she would be rehearsing two plays in tandem while performing a third. As a consequence she played Cleopatra in *My Fair Lady* and Ibsen's tragic heroine Hedda Gabler in *No Sex Please, We're British*, in which she was said to have given the part a 'robustly comic interpretation'. After twenty years in the profession she was, as you may imagine, delighted to be nominated in the Daily Star Drama Awards as Most Promising Newcomer. (In the event she narrowly lost out to Bagpuss).

Shag

It's hard to believe that Aalison Aaronson (her real name by the way is Brenda Thomas but she changed it in order to appear as the first entry in *Spotlight,* the actor's directory) has only been in 'the business', as she calls it, for a mere two years. She has already worked in over 37 different rep. companies on the North East coast alone – staying as long as a month in some of them. She has starred in Samuel Beckett's *Happy Days*, a one-woman play for which she was nominated in the *Alnick*

Radio Active Rep.: the first radio broadcast of La Cage aux Folles

IN REHEARSAL
A Typical Day

12.0 The first actor arrives, Jeremy Bottoms. Waits five minutes, assumes he must be early and so goes over to the pub for a quick drink.

12.10 Director Edward Maliphant arrives, finds no-one there and goes off to look for them in the canteen.

12.20 Actor Frederick Dodd arrives, sees the room empty, and assumes everyone must have gone on somewhere else. And so leaves a note.

12.25 Director Edward Maliphant returns from the canteen to find a note from Frederick Dodd asking where they've all gone. Slightly confused, he goes off to phone him.

12.30 Jeremy Bottoms returns from the pub and, seeing nobody, assumes he's still early and so goes back for another quick drink.

12.45 Director Edward Maliphant returns once again from having rung Frederick Dodd and found him out, and decides to try the pub.

12.50 Actress Amanda Smidgeon arrives having spent 10 minutes driving there and 50 minutes finding a parking space. She decides to ring director Edward Maliphant to find out where everyone is and so goes off to find a phone.

12.55 Edward returns from the pub having found Jeremy Bottoms along with the fifth actor Ian Polgate, who has been in the pub since 12 o'clock, claiming he thought that was where they were supposed to meet.

1.50 Amanda returns having spent 15 minutes finding a phone-box that worked, another 15 finding a Post Office to buy a phone card, another 15 queuing up in the Post Office to get one, and another 15 listening to Edward's ansaphone message.

2.45 Frederick Dodd arrives having driven 30 miles home and found a message on his ansaphone from Edward Maliphant telling him to come back immediately.

3.0 So the day gets off to a flying start, and they are ready to begin reading.

Advertiser as Best Supporting Actress. Her most cherished theatrical ambition is one day to star in *The Mousetrap.*

Amanda Smidgeon is a delightfully robust and friendly member of the rep. who is, as she says, 'Proud to be Merry'. She is always to be found with a pipe in her mouth and a packet of tobacco in her waistcoat pocket which she is more than ready to share with one of the other girls in the rep. 'Shag anybody?' has become quite her catch-phrase in the ladies' cloakroom. She made her mark on the stage as one of the youngest ever King Lears, and *Radio Active* regulars will no doubt be surprised to learn that she is the voice behind Sally, the husky-voiced 10-year-old in our serial *Mrs Naylor's Notebook,* and also Simon, the husky voiced castrato in our drama series chronicling the lives of the early Christian leaders, *Pick of the Popes.*

Ian Polgate joined the rep. after sending us an extremely amusing letter in which he said we were his last chance and offered to work for free and wash dishes if we gave him a job! He can now be heard giving his distinctive 'Hear, hear' or 'This way, sir' in most rep. productions, except when he is working in the canteen.

No Denying

But whatever their failings, there's no denying that the Radio Active Repertory Company have become an institution. Rather like Broadmoor, and with much the same problems.

But at the end of the day, what does their latest director Edward Maliphant make of them? He told us: 'I think there's been a lot of bad press and a lot of adverse criticism behind their back. And I think that's wrong. The only way you're going to get them to buck their ideas up is to tell it to their faces'.

Sound Effects

NIGEL PRY has been responsible for the sound effects For Radio Rep, if responsible is the word, ever since he began at the station, and his success rate is extraordinary. Complete failure to reproduce even the simplest sounds.

He has his own reasons for why this should be:

'Well, yes man Pry certainly and what are literally sound effects now here, bang and crashing all about, really much the better for it', and they will remain his own reasons until someone manages to interpret them.

REUBEN: Tes right cold, Joan.

JOAN: Ahhhh Reuben. Wind up the shutters.

FX   WINDOW CLOSED

FX   DOOR KNOCK. DOOR OPEN

REUBEN: Wull, wull, wull, look ochh art ere.

JOAN: Oohh art et, Reuben?

REUBEN: Art moi sun Jed.

JED: Tes roight en sez yer en ner merstick, farter.

REUBEN: Dis tis yor Aunt Joan, Jed.

JED: Oi dern tink I member er, Dad.

REUBEN: Cos dem dus Jed. En dis ert her sun Gabby wot ert returned erter ull dis tim.

JED: Noooooooaaahhhhhh?

REUBEN: Arrrrr.

JED: Nooooahhhhhhhh.

REUBEN: Arrrrrrrr!

GABBY: Arrrrrrrrrrrrrrrrrrrr, Jed.
            I be Gabby, returned ter my mother and to the place wert I
            have loved all thes yers, returned as a traveller who has
            experienced much abroad but one who has learnt that though
            the the werld has much to offer, in the end all a man can ever
            want is in his own back yard. Welcome my old and new friends.
            Welcome all.
            (BREAKS DOWN IN TEARS OF MIXED HAPPINESS AND SADNESS)

GRAMS   CLOSING MUSIC

The big speech — give it the full welly!!

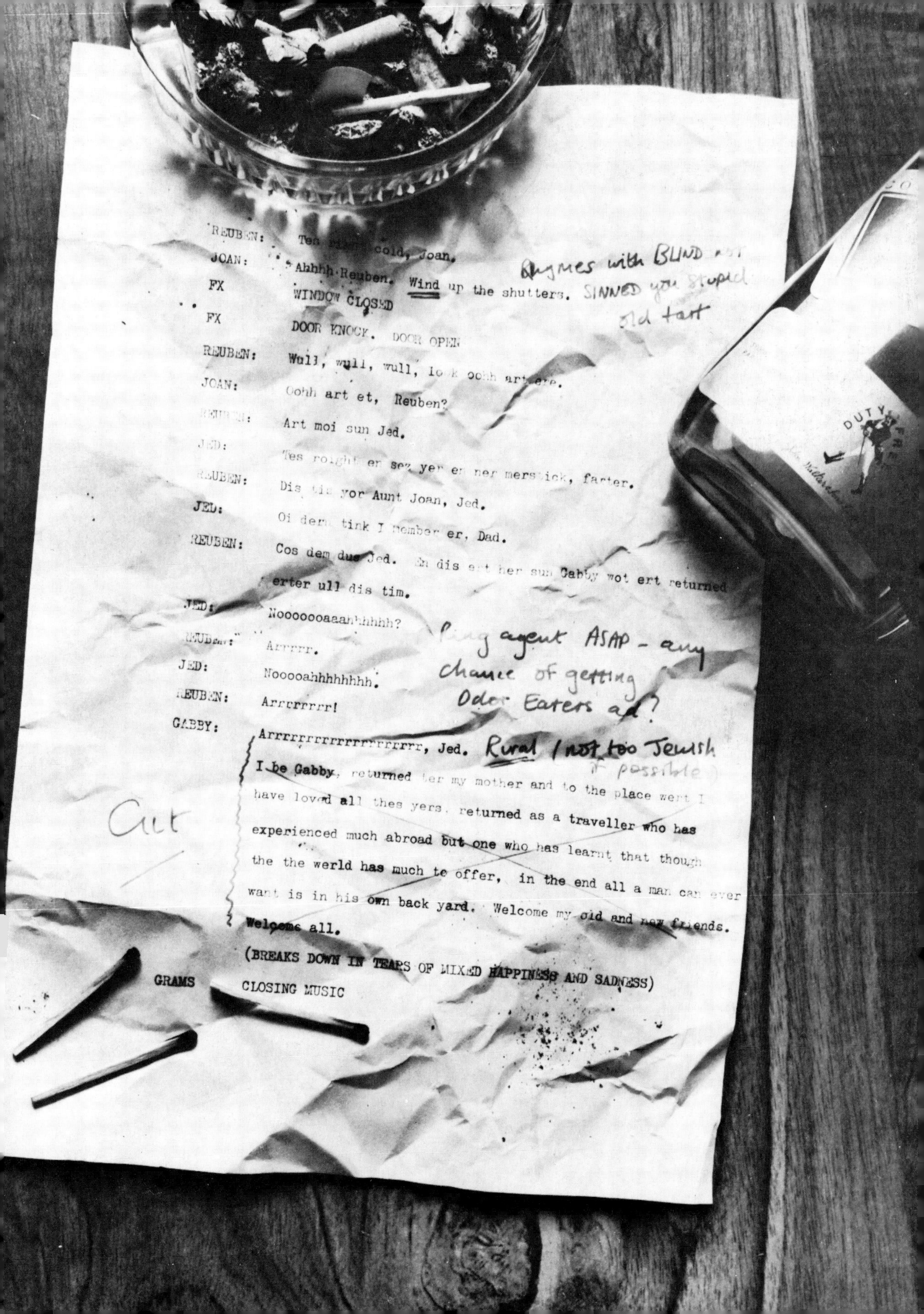

REUBEN: Ten ... cold, Joan.

JOAN: Ahhhh Reuben. Wind up the shutters.

FX   WINDOW CLOSED

FX   DOOR KNOCK. DOOR OPEN

REUBEN: Wull, wull, wull, look ooh art ere.

JOAN: Oohh art et, Reuben?

REUBEN: Art moi sun Jed.

JED: Tes roight er sez yer er ner merstick, farter.

REUBEN: Dis tis yor Aunt Joan, Jed.

JED: Oi dern tink I member er, Dad.

REUBEN: Cos dem dus Jed. En dis ert her sun Gabby wot ert returned erter ull dis tim.

JED: Nooooooaaahhhhh?

REUBEN: Arrrrr.

JED: Nooooahhhhhhhh.

REUBEN: Arrrrrrrr!

GABBY: Arrrrrrrrrrrrrrrrrrrr, Jed. I be Gabby, returned ter my mother and to the place wert I have loved all thes yers. returned as a traveller who has experienced much abroad but one who has learnt that though the the werld has much te offer, in the end all a man can ever want is in his own back yard. Welcome my old and new friends. Welcome all.

          (BREAKS DOWN IN TEARS OF MIXED HAPPINESS AND SADNESS)

GRAMS   CLOSING MUSIC

Handwritten annotations:

Rhymes with BLIND not SINNED you stupid old tart

Ring agent ASAP - any chance of getting Odor Eaters ad?

Rural (not too Jewish if possible)

Cut

TWENTY-FOUR HOURS OF *Nigel Pry*

EACH DAY Nigel Pry walks all the 17 miles to the studios here at Radio Active and 17 miles home again at night. All this in the face of often treacherous weather and in spite of a regular bus and train service.

The reason is that Nigel is clinically insane.

Each week we look at a typical day in the life of a famous celebrity, but this week it's the turn of Nigel Pry, highly abused and critically panned reporter for Radio Active

The Nigel Pry Show Friday 7.15

At night, when his colleagues like to sleep tucked up in their beds, Nigel goes hill-walking. The South Downs are at their most beautiful at night, and Nigel attempts to recapture their beauty on his Kodak Instamatic.

Nigel Pry: Photographer

Chanctonbury Ring, Sussex

Nigel Pry: Patient

Described simply by his doctors as 'tonto', Nigel has been certified for the past 20 years.

At midday, Nigel jogs fully 8 miles to a roadside cafe, despite the station's canteen and bar. Moreover Nigel considers it well worthwhile even though this cafe is officially described by the AA as 'derelict'.

Nigel began his career at Radio Active as a newsreader – a job normally associated with sitting down. But cocking a snook at convention, Nigel prefers to suspend himself from the studio ceiling.

But his audience figures are second to none. His show is consistently the most unpopular programme on radio.

Nigel Pry: Newsreader

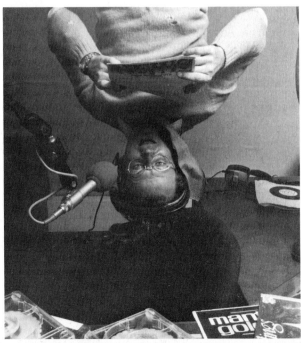

Most nights Nigel goes potholing. Sometimes he'll stay down there for two, three, even four days, or at least until the rescue services can find him.

Nigel realises that his lifestyle is not everyone's cup of tea. Nigel has not slept, for example, since 1965. And even then it was under anaesthetic at the dentist. But you won't catch Nigel complaining. Nor will you catch him rejoicing. For Nigel has not strung a coherent sentence together in his life.

But still he smiles, for Nigel doesn't know what un happiness means. Nor indeed what happiness means, or motor car, or cat, or yes or no. In fact, Nigel appears to have no conception of language as we know it. But life goes on and with it Nigel Pry. On this week's programme, we ask the question, 'Why?' ■

NOW!
A portable phone
that truly fits
in your pocket!

Honest Ron's Cellular phone

SPECIAL FEATURES:

- Comes complete with 25 miles of cord
- No need for batteries; just plug straight in
- Easy to clean
- Finger-sized dialling holes
- One-level volume control
- Doesn't make messes around the house
- Enables you to both make <u>and</u> receive phone calls
- That's about it for special features

Radio Active: Appealing to Everyone

Last year saw the first Radio Active Radiothon in aid of the 'Help A Local Pensioner' Appeal. Over £900,000 was raised, and as a result, that pensioner now lives in a country mansion near Windsor

THIS YEAR our 'Help A Local Junkie' Appeal aims to supply a million pounds' worth of hard drugs to the needy.

Here are some of the highlights of last year's Radiothon.

Sponsorships

Italian restaurateur, Alfredo Wilkins of Coventry, was sponsored to make the longest piece of spaghetti ever recorded!

Unfortunately, the Children's Sponsored Cycle Race passed through that way on its route and five children were sadly garotted. Still, as Alfredo said, 'That's showbiz!'

Auctions in the Foyer

Many celebrities magnanimously donated some of their personal possessions.

**RADIOTHON
Sunday 6am-6pm**

Nigel Pry explores a way of doubling the profit on the sale of a Turner oil painting, with Charlotte Chestnut of Christie's looking on.

Elsie Tanner's toothbrush

Chas & Dave's socks

John Inman's toe-nail

David Hamilton's eyelash

Generous Donations

The general public's generosity was overwhelming

Ransoms

With only half-an-hour to go, we were still £899,850 short of our target of £900,000. Until, right at the death, Nigel Pry stepped in and very kindly kidnapped four children for us.

Within minutes the parents had coughed up the ransoms which allowed Radio Active to reach its target of £900,000! While Sir Norman Tonsil was personally delighted to have reached his target of £950,000 from the advertising revenue. ■

A Truly Criminal Show

Each week Radio Active does its bit for the world of crime, with 'Stop That Crime ...'

**Stop That Crime ... UK
Thursday 9.25pm
Up-date Wednesday 9.25pm**

OVER the last week, there have been literally hundreds of calls from people, saying that after our detailed reconstruction of a car theft in Bolton, they've had their cars stolen in exactly the same way. Sometimes our crime reconstructions can be shocking and upsetting to listeners, as in last week's when Frederick Dodd's performance as the old man was particularly bad. Also last week, listeners will have heard a police officer asking you to phone in if you thought your house might be inadequately protected against burglary. This week, with your help, police are hoping to find the man who impersonated that officer and who is thought to be responsible for a sudden outbreak of burglaries around the country.

Up-date . . .

Following last week's dramatisation of a burglary on a caravan site in the West Country, narrated by Mike Channel, the **Stop That Crime** switchboard has been flooded with helpful suggestions:

Mrs Dorothy Kinsman of Berkshire rang to suggest: 'The man who was called "Ted" might well be someone called Edward, as it's quite a popular abbreviation with the lower classes.'

Edwin Boyd phoned to say he'd just returned from a caravan holiday in the West Country, so could one of the burglars have possibly been him?

And *Sonia Howie* called to say she thought she recognised one of the voices as being that of Mike Channel, who she says, 'used to be a radio broadcaster in the 1960s, but I'm not sure what he's doing now.'

This week Police will be asking listeners' help in solving a murder in Southwark which took place last Friday. They'll be asking any listener, if he is the murderer, to phone in and give himself up.

Also still on the WANTED list are:

Mario D'Arcy, mastermind behind the 'fruit machine' protection racket, wanted for questioning in connection with the whereabouts of four missing knee-caps.

This is an artist's impression of him.

Also wanted is another artist.

John 'Hardman' Daley, wanted for assault and intent to cause grievous bodily harm whilst stealing his four-year-old son's piggy bank. A police description runs as follows: pink, with a squiggley tail and a slit along the top of its back. A police description of the wanted man is as follows: a ruddy complexion under his sodding hair and between his bloody ears. ∎

OUT TO LAUNCH

Radio Active salutes the launch of Britain's first space rocket

**Britain's First Space Rocket
Thursday 11am**

AFTER 20 YEARS of research Britain has developed its very own space rocket. The final problem, which has occupied scientists for the last few years, has now been overcome, and they have designed the perfect launching pad, with the technical assistance of the Milk Marketing Board.

The state-of-the-art rocket is over 500 feet high, is capable of withstanding pressure up to 10,000Gs, and requires a crew of 14 people to strike the 10-foot match against the 20-foot matchbox.

The only thing that can stop the launch going ahead is a sudden shower of rain, in which case the Prime Minister, the American Defense Secretary and the various Commonwealth heads will go inside for soup and hot chocolate, and we will broadcast a repeat of Trouser Experience in Concert (*first transmitted Thursday 11.0am*). ∎

Blue Flash – Britain's first space rocket

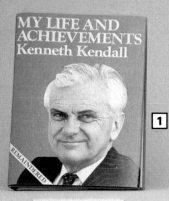

MY LIFE AND ACHIEVEMENTS
Kenneth Kendall

REMAINDERED

1

THE SHELL MOTORING ATLAS OF SARK

2

THE OBSERVER BOOK OF Boiled Eggs

Adults Only

With illustrations

6

GOOD FOOD GUIDE 1952

7

Abseiling for the Elderly

A step-by-step guide

EXIT

9

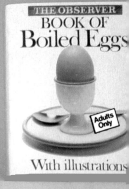

The Do-It-Yourself Book

SEXUALLY EXPLICIT

Eighty-six pages of blank paper

4

HALIFAX A-Z

Every street, every alley

Geographers' A-Z Map Company

8

INDOOR GARDENING
Cecily Deayton

3

10

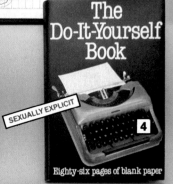

LOTS OF SEXY PHOTOS

An Educational Study

THE FAMILY ENCYCLOPAEDIA OF MECHANICAL ENGINEERING

MAHO MH 600 E

All you need to know about this tricky subject

5

Paula Yates'
ROCK STARS ON THE TOILET

BOOK OF THE MONTH

Please accept my application to become a member of the Useless Book Club and send me the 3 introductory books whose numbers I have written below PLUS the Book of the Month **Rock Stars on the Toilet**, whether I want it or not and which I realise might offend me. If I am not completely satisfied I may return the books within 10 days and will owe nothing but the full retail price of each book. As a member, I do not need to purchase an average of one book per month, but I shall however buy at least 12 books in each year of my membership.

NAME ....

ADDRESS ....

....

THE **Useless Book** CLUB

IT'S HEALING TIME!

★ ★

This week's host is the Man with the Host, the Right Reverend Billy B. Wainwright the Third (sponsored by Uncle Bob's Deep Fried Turkey Pieces)

American Gospel Show Thursday 11.0

THE Rev. Billy Wainwright flew in specially across the Atlantic to present these programmes. He told our reporter about his broadcasts. 'I'm delighted this Thursday to be able to bring you the word straight from the man himself through God's chosen gift, Radio Active, 89.3 on the FM dial, which is God's chosen frequency.

'Yes, God will be coming through your radio this Thursday and he'll be saying to you: "If you've got a sick loved one around the house, a sick child, or a sick senior citizen who can no longer control their bodily functions maybe, or even a little sick pet, then just bring it right up next to your radio this Thursday and stick its little sick part up against the speaker." Yes, this Thursday, God wants you to take that bandaged head or surgical stocking, and he wants you to press it hard against your radio and that sick part will be healed. Last week you may remember we heard from little Billy Martin in Liverpool who was a cripple. You may remember we heard him take his first steps in fifteen years as we gave him the will power during my show to get across the room and turn off his radio.

'So, tune in for more miracles this week. But don't forget that God's miracles don't come for nothing. So God wants you to take out your cheque book and write out a sum of money that magnifies the Lord in the Glory of all its noughts. So write out that cheque and send it to

A little sick part

the following address, and by the way, don't you forget that all of God's children just love the taste of Uncle Bob's Deep Fried Turkey Pieces.

'Send you cheques to: God, c/o His Trusted Bank Manager on Earth, The Reverend Billy B. Wainwright the Third, "Chez The Lord", The Cayman Islands'. ∎

OH, WHAT A LOVELY

On Thursday, Radio Active turns back the clock of time and journeys down memory lane, recalling some of the fun times of June 1944 and playing some of the top sounds around at the time.
Plus there's a chance to win a special Radio Active souvenir piece of shrapnel by seeing how many words you can make out of D-Day

The D-Day Show
Thursday 11.0

THE SECOND WORLD WAR wasn't all fun and games. There was a serious side to it. Many people, for example, remember the fighting that went on between Germany and the Allied Forces.

On Thursday, Radio Active broadcasts its own special commemoration of the Normandy Invasion.

All the Radio Active D.J.'s will be out and about, doing their bit for this special one-off never-to-be-repeated show, which can incidentally be heard again at the same time next week. 'Oh so daring' Mike Hunt will be taking a party of kids on an exact re-enactment of the D-Day Landings, including everything from crossing the Channel on an Army landing craft, to repelling hundreds of holiday-makers off the beaches and driving them up the cliffs, and finally finishing off with some authentic precision bombing of key targets.

Our Norwegian disc-jockey, Oivind Vinstra, will also be joining in as he has his own reasons for remembering D-Day. 'Mange ya ogsa por arbeid die Mattemude tak ettospart, ya ya, ogsa beide ya hodsleden in Lillehammer, ut die Norske por ya utsa met Trondheim.'

And they will remain his own reasons until someone manages to interpret them.

And Martin Brown has sadly been given the job of compiling his own potted history of D-Day, which he had only got half way through at the time of going to press.

Listeners to the programme can hear the rest of that potted history of D-Day, taking in the American War of Independence and Russian invasion of Afghanistan.

Our guest on Thursday's show will be Colonel Brian 'Jumbo' Bartlett who will be reminiscing about his war-time companions including General 'Large Hooter' Barnes-Boothby and Wing Commander 'Nocturnal Emission' Smith. Also he will be talking about his book, *Oh What A Lovely D-Day*, in which he outlines the various invasion plans that were considered.

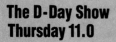

Potted: Martin Brown's version of D-Day

CHAPTER 14

OVER THE TOP

WE started with two plans of attack. The first involved the construction of a Channel Tunnel. This sadly foundered on the impossibility of getting the Germans to agree a cost and starting date at their end. So, to soften them up, we launched 'the bouncing bomb' – a bomb which bounced over their first line of defence and did not burst immediately on impact. Unfortunately, it did not burst at all, and was last seen bouncing off towards Australia. At least, we felt, it was not entirely wasted.

Our thoughts then turned to electrical warfare. The plan was to pick a day when the entire Germany army was swimming off the coast of France, and then drop into the Channel an enormous electric fire connected to all the power stations in the country. This plan was sadly rejected at the last minute.

After some thought, I myself came up with a bold, exciting plan of my own. It was based on the Battle of Hastings. It had worked before, and above all it had the great advantage that Hastings was in this country, thereby making the whole invasion thing a great deal easier. We wouldn't have to cross the Channel or enter into combat with the Germans, whom many of us at the time thought to be frankly hostile to us. Plus it had the crucial element of surprise. No-one in Hastings would be expecting it. Sadly, however, I was unable actually to submit this plan, as at that time I was under severe confinement in Broadmoor.

173

The D-Day Show will also be bringing you some of the exciting wartime bulletins from the Ministry of Information

Also joining the Radio Active team will be American songwriter Yip Wallensky, the man responsible for the song that for millions epitomised Britain during the war: *There'll be Bluebirds over the White Cliffs of Dover.* The fact that there have never actually been any bluebirds outside of America seems to be an inaccuracy that is echoed in the remainder of the original lyric, as can be seen from a copy of the manuscript after it was corrected by the publishers:

THERE'LL BE BLUEBIRDS OVER THE WHITE CLIFFS OF DOVER

TOMORROW JUST YOU WAIT AND SEE

THERE'LL BE BUFFALO ROAMING JUST OUTSIDE GODALMING *fun and laughter, and peace ever after*

THERE'LL BE BLUEBERRY FLAPJACKS AND PEPSI *blue birds over*

AND GOLF SLACKS *The White cliffs of Dover*

TOMORROW JUST YOU WAIT AND SEE

THE SHEPHERD WILL TEND HIS SHEEP

THE CACTUS WILL BLOOM AGAIN *valley*

AND ENGLAND WILL GO TO SLEEP *Jimmy*

AND WE'LL PROBABLY HAVE TO BAIL YOU LIMEYS OUT AGAIN *In his own little room again*

JUST LIKE WE DID IN THE LAST WAR

TWO THINGS TO BEAR IN MIND AT ALL TIMES

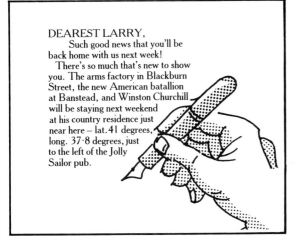

DEAREST LARRY,
Such good news that you'll be back home with us next week!
There's so much that's new to show you. The arms factory in Blackburn Street, the new American batallion at Banstead, and Winston Churchill will be staying next weekend at his country residence just near here – lat. 41 degrees, long. 37·8 degrees, just to the left of the Jolly Sailor pub.

When writing to a loved one or sweetheart, be careful what you say!

SHOPKEEPER:
Can I help you, sir?

CUSTOMER:
Zwei Kugelschreiber und ein Schallplatterspieler, bitte.

And keep your ears open for anyone sounding suspicious.

Children of the Wirral

Over the next six weeks Radio Active Times will be publishing in its entirety the new best-selling pop biography, by writer and author, Bud Houston

PART ONE: BEFORE THE BEGINNING

MEGALITHIC. No other word more readily springs to mind, when one thinks of the life-long success of the Hee Bee Gee Bees. Even such words as 'epic', 'gargantuan' or 'existential', barely come anywhere near describing accurately the influence these three brothers have had on the pop music world. 'Great', 'extensive', or 'very large indeed', in a similar way, simply don't cover half of it. And as for 'major',

'sizable' or 'pretty damn big', well, you can just leave them out altogether – they're laughable understatements.

For who is not familiar with the names of Dobbin, Norris and Garry Cribb? Quite obviously, almost no-one is, but that's probably because they're better known as the 'Hee Bee Gee Bees', quite simply the most successful pop phenomenon in the

history of modern music, the contemporary arts and, of course, pop phenomena.

It has been said that the Hee Bee Gee Bees are the Greek Gods of the pop world: Norris – Poseidon, Dobbin – Athena, and Garry, by his own confession, Zeus. Nor would the brothers themselves poo-poo such an analogy. Indeed, it was they who first suggested it. And it is with

this same self-effacing humility that they approach their work, as they seek to produce that 'inimitable' Hee Bee Gee Bees sound – the soundtrack of our times, the epitome of all that is admirable and excellent in the world today, as they put it.

But the story of the Hee Bee Gee Bees is more than just the modest account of hit records, international superstardom, and unbridled genius. For this is a family chronicle telling warmly of the loves and triumphs, the affairs and romances, and the divorces and law-suits, that have filled

Norris, Dobbin, Garry

their lives as they have our newspapers.

The brothers began singing and making music at a staggeringly early age. Norris wrote one of their earlier hits, *Now I've Found That the Earth is Round,* just after his first Geography lesson, and Dobbin, his twin, penned the million-selling *Worms* on his second birthday. Several years earlier, Garry had baffled medical science by being the first baby to speak from the womb, when he asked for more manuscript paper.

Success came thick and fast for the boys, and they were already international celebrities and millionaires by their second year at primary school. Moreover, in their teens and subsequent late-teens, they created a body of work that is

enough to put the name of the Cribb Brothers quite justifiably alongside those of the great composers: Bach, Beethoven, Mozart, Manilow – all can be seen, in some measure, in the works of these three homely, self-confessed 'legends in their own lifetime'.

But their initial world-wide breakthrough that began back in the '60's wasn't kind to the Hee Bee Gee Bees, and they suffered a series of split-ups, breakdowns, shake-ups, break-ups and split-downs, before re-emerging in 1975, feeling slightly sick. Nevertheless, their re-emergence, now under the instigation of their new manager, Robert Stigwig, and the overwhelming success of the soundtrack album *Friday Evening Disease,* turned the Hee Bee Gee Bees into the phenomenon of the decade. Many have seen it as rivalling the German invasion of Poland in international significance, and as being tantamount to a nuclear holo-

caust in terms of its devastating effect on the world population. Who can say? For Garry, admittedly, it was 'just a good laugh'.

The sales figures for the *Evening Disease* album were enormous. As were those of the singles taken from that album, *Stayin' Awake, Chive Talking* and the now classic *How Deep Is Your Mouth?* Their subsequent album, *Water Having Passed,* also went gold, this time within 90 minutes of being released, and everyone, it seemed, had become a Hee Bee Gee Bees fan overnight. Their music helped bridge the yawning chasms between music followers, so that their audience included people of all ages, colours, creeds and chest sizes.

Indeed, it is from this sense of unity and oneness that the true message of their music comes. Nowhere is it more poetically and succinctly put than in one of the lines of their hit single, *Meaningless*

Songs in Very High Voices, where Dobbin tells us, 'Love is better than hate'. Such profundity is rare in the average pop lyric.

How much, then, does the world owe to the lyrics of the Hee Bee Gee Bees? How large is our debt? Clearly, 'enormous' is not the word. Nor indeed would 'gargantuan' be, or 'epic', or 'existential' – but that's another story.

Suffice it to say, the three brothers have reached a status of unusually high proportions in the world today, and in the following five weeks we hope to trace their journey through life: from childhood, through adolescence, on to manhood, immortality, and finally, of course, omniscient deity. Appropriately enough, our story begins in Macclesfield, England . . . ∎

Next week – Part Two: Starting to Begin

FLEX'S FILHARMONIC FAVES!

Starting this Wednesday Radio Active will be bringing you a little high culture, and regular listeners will know that means one thing – our franchise is coming up for renewal

Classical Music Show Wednesday 4.0

THERE IS no one better to host our classical music hour than Mike Flex, who will be with you all week, or at least until we run out of our library's supply of classical records.

Mike Flex writes: Yes, what a week I've got for you, a real chance for you to clap along to the classics. And a great thrill for me to be presenting this show, which features some of my all time filharmonic faves, some of which I have even heard all the way through. And what better way to start on Monday than with Ludwig van Beethoven's Fifth Symphony.

Now, one thing I must warn you about in advance. This isn't the actual recording with Beethoven himself on it. I was a bit disappointed when I heard it to realise that these are just session musicians, rather like the Bay City Rollers, but not quite as original. But I gather that Beethoven doesn't actually play on many of his records these days, so perhaps we shouldn't be too surprised. I think he's rather busy writing music for things like the butter ads. However, I believe he may well be touring later on in the year so look out for him then.

On Tuesday, it's the turn of Dvorak, the guy who writes the bread ads, and I'm delighted to say that we will actually be playing that famous music from one of them, which also goes by the name of the *New World Symphony*, apparently. Wednesday, it's the turn of Les Sylphides, who will be giving us his *Chopin*. From the album sleeve I'm afraid I can't find out too much about Les but I gather that this *Chopin* is a bit of dance music, so get on down and strut your funky stuff to that.

On Thursday it's a real classic, perhaps the most powerful piece of classical music ever written, Mike Oldfield's *Tubular Bells*.

Which is more, I'm afraid, than can be said for our final classical offering on Friday, Handel's *Messiah*. At least they've thoughtfully printed the lyrics on the sleeve (unlike Ludo and Les by the way), but I'm afraid lines like 'Her warfare is accomplished that her iniquity is pardoned' smack to me of some of the worst excesses of Rick Wakeman. And at least Rick has a few synthesisers to play with. The brief snatch I heard of this sounds just like a lot of acoustic instruments. Can't they afford to pay their electricity bill? And, what is more, everyone sounds like they're singing different things half the time. All in all, a pretty tacky, low-budget sound I'm afraid . . . but maybe the *Messiahs* will get it together a bit in the future, particularly if they can get some one who really knows about music, like Dave Stewart of the Eurythmics, to produce them.

Anyway, that's the line up of this week's Classic Classics. And don't worry if you find that the music doesn't really grab you, because during some of the slower bits we'll be having all our usual phone-ins and competitions. ∎

RADIO FIRSTS

A sparkling, brand new radio series of television spin offs

Yes RADIO ACTIVE brings you the very latest in creative broadcasting – a series of clapped out old television quiz and game shows specially adapted for radio by taking away the pictures.

Which Baby are You?

Each week we'll be picking a different child of Swedish star, Britt Orkland, and the contestants have to try and guess who the father is. ■

Give Us a Clue

The hilarious charades game which makes perfect radio because you're not allowed to talk!

Thursday 11.0 am

**This week's baby . . .
(His daddy is not a singer, so perhaps it's Rod Stewart?)**

If you have a small child,
and live near a motorway,
DON'T let him sit out in it!

Putting small children in the fast lane
of a motorway is dangerous — DON'T DO IT!

A BLINDINGLY OBVIOUS PUBLIC INFORMATION ADVERTISEMENT

Where Have All the Flowers Gone?

An investigation into what happened to the Hippies of '68

IN 1968 Zoe and Jesus helped run a commune in Cornwall. Now, exactly 18½ years later they are still there. On this fascinating (if occasionally turgid and frequently boring programme) we will set out to find if they have changed at all. Mike Flex took an all-expenses-paid trip to St Ives to see them.

Where Are They Now?   Thursday 11.0

Zoe and Jesus (Maureen and George)

Zoe and Jesus now prefer to be known as Maureen and George, but they are delighted that the commune is still going after all these years. Of course, they have had to adapt slightly with the times. Nowadays, for instance, the squatters are called 'Residents' and they each pay £25 a night, but Maureen thinks that it's worth it because everyone now has their own room which is much nicer than the old days. They have also had the wall of the communal living space knocked through and they have made a rather nice little patio surrounded by begonias which match the patio furniture (sadly the chairs are only for show and not for sitting on).

George still practises Transcendental Meditation, although now he calls it his afternoon nap. Maureen is still into grass, which she cuts religiously every Saturday morning and stores in plastic sacks to make compost for her geranium bed.

They admit that they still see a good deal of the police, but only because they now hold the annual police ball in their guest house. They are still into all the sounds — Clapton, the Beatles — in fact whatever Jimmy Young has on. So time has stood still here. As long as they have the requisite £25 a week and they wipe their feet when they come in anyone is welcome — anyone that is except animals, children and members of the hippy convoy.

Some of the children of the Sixties have followed a different path as Mike Channel reports from his no-expenses trip to Coventry.

A complete Softie

In 1968 Sandra Perkins adopted the name Rishiba Ajita Sumati Vimala Sitala, Flower of the Sun. And since that time she has been a devoted follower of the Reverend Man Yung Soft.

She is a Softie.

She first heard about the Softies when she was working at the checkout counter of Sainsbury's. A wide-eyed smiling man, who she later found had left without paying, told her about the Sri Krishna Ashram, the focal point for their followers and all true pilgrims of love, which was situated just outside Coventry. She immediately realised that this was the direction she wanted her life to go in, and so she just dropped everything — at the time half a dozen eggs and a bottle of White's lemonade which was docked from her final pay packet.

On her arrival at the ashram she was met at the gate by a disciple dressed in a simple white gown. He told her that all she needed was love and he asked her to give him all her worldly belongings, which she did. She never saw him again.

She has lived in the ashram ever since and says that she has never wanted to leave this haven of peace. Not that she could anyway with the electric fence, the searchlights and the land mines, but she insists that that is not the point. Her days are taken up with meditation and her daily tasks. Her task is working eight hours a day in the ashram wholefood shop. A complete change from her former life in Sainsbury's.

At the end of each day she has a simple vegetarian meal sitting on a bare floor eating brown rice and yoghurt from a plain wooden bowl (£5.50 plus VAT).

She's sorry that her parents have had to sell their house in order to keep her there but she hopes they can understand that she has dedicated her life to the Reverend Soft. She is truly a Softie in the heart, a Softie in the soul and, above all, a Softie in the head. ∎

Records Slashed!

Classic Records at Classic Prices

THE PEE CEES
TRIPLE SIDE
TOO DEPRESSED TO COMMIT SUICIDE

£1.99

Purple Pants Ponce

£0.09

StatusQuid
BORING SONG

£0.99

£0.49

FRANKIE GOES TO THE BANK

JACK MICHAELSON

Rock Bottom Records at Rock Bottom Prices

PLUS lots more old favourites you thought you'd seen the last of:

843	**HUMAN LEAK**	I Don't Want Your Baby
592	**DURHAM DURHAM**	Pretty Boys on Video
227	**PAUL YUK**	Wherever I Lay My Hat, That's My Hatstand
000	**BLACK LICE**	Shagadoo
716	**GARY INHUMAN**	Are Trains Electric?
238	**SUPERTRASH**	Scatalogical Song
387	**CARY CLITTER**	Cary Clitter is Back
126	**WIZENED**	Thank Christ It Isn't Christmas Every Day
745	**U-Huh**	Hunting Lino
930	**PHALCO**	Rock Me Beckenbauer

Dave Witherby

I Saw George Michael'

Some of the schoolfriends of today's pop singers talk about the stars as they remember them

Schoolfriends of the Stars Thursday 11.0

SOME of the nonentities featured in this week's programme told *Radio Active Times* of their early acquaintance with the famous. First, Dave Witherby, who was a primary school chum of George Michael.

Dave Witherby

'Oh yes, I remember my old mate George very well. We were inseparable in those days. I remember in particular one day when he came up to me in the playground and said, "How about a game of conkers then Dave?" And I said to him, "Now listen George, don't you go wasting your time playing conkers, you concentrate on your song-writing and who knows, one day, you might have a number

one hit with a song called *Careless Whispers* – just to pick a name at random." And he said, "Thanks very much for the advice Dave, I'll do that right away ... *Careless Whispers* you say?", and he turned to go back to the music room and walked straight into my other great friend Andrew Ridgely. Wham! Just like that, and I said, "Hey, George, that would be a great name for a group, wouldn't it, and you couldn't find a better person to be in that group which I've all on the spur of the moment suggested that you call Wham! than my great friend Andrew Ridgely who you have never met before, but who I think you might have a very successful partnership with until you decide to split up in about the middle of 1986 taking a date at random."

'And George said, "Well, Dave, I must say you seem to be full of splendid ideas, why don't you come

and be in this group that you have so brilliantly thought of a name for?" and I said, "No thank you, George, I'm afraid I've already set my heart on becoming a council drainage inspector in Bushey, and being an international superstar and multi-millionaire would just get in the way."

'And that's what I'm doing now, but I'm very pleased George decided to follow my advice.'

Simon Boswell

'I suppose you could say I had a bit of influence on my best friend becoming what he is today. He was this little pudgy faced kid who was always playing the piano and he was thinking of going into the music business. And I said to him, "Well, you can't become a rock star with a name like yours. Let's face it, Elton John sounds ridiculous. Why don't you change it to Reg Dwight?" Well, he took my advice and now he runs his very own pie and eel shop in the East End. Reg's Pie and Eels. Doing very well too, I believe.'

George Michael (I think)

Conkers

Colin Trott

'Well, of course they weren't called Diana Ross and the Supremes when I knew them. They were just three ordinary blokes from Newcastle-Under-Lyme called Phil, Winkle and Nobby. But I knew as soon as they came on the telly in 1966 that they'd now become Diana Ross and the Supremes. I'm just sorry that I lost my hearing and eyesight in 1965.' ■

Colin Trott

Diana Ross & The Supremes

A Word from God

This week's brief message comes from Radio Active's resident vicar, the Rt. Reverend, Rev. Wright

YOU KNOW, it's all very easy, isn't it, to say that religion is only an esoteric ecclesiastic anachronism. But really, it's not that simple.

Because, although religion is about seriousness and solemnity and sadness and suffering, it's also about happiness and joy and cheerfulness and mirth. About jollity and goodwill and fun and rejoicing, about hope and optimism and pleasure and enjoyment. And celebration and gladness and contentment and satisfaction.

About delight and rapture and bliss and ecstacy, and blessedness and harmony and comfort and

(cont. p.35)

The Radio Active Times

The editor of the *Radio Active Times* would like to apologise to the following for the inconvenience caused them and their families by the staff of the station during the production of this publication, and hopes that they will soon be on their feet again: Alice Adamson, Nicky Adamson, John Armitstead, Christopher Brace, Mr & Mrs M. Davis, Mike Edwards, Kate Fraser, Ros Graves, Alex Gloth, David Grove and St George's Hospital Radio 9, David and Sarah Hardy, Daisy Hayden, Stephen Ibbotson, Sally Ingram, June Kelly, Christopher Lee, Liz & Clive Leverton, Paul Mayhew-Archer, Mo Chaos & Nobby, Jimmy Mulville, Elisabetta Nicolello i Amice, Jack Perkins, Lisa Perkins, Chris Richardson, Jamie Rix, David Tyler, and Coco Wake-Porter. Also to: Capital Radio; John Davies Picture Framing; Express Dairies, Morden; Orchard Restaurant, Belsize Park; BBC Hulton Picture Library; Camera Press – David Bailey, Ray Hamilton, David Linton, Snowdon, Alan Wicker; Island Records; Radio Times; Topham. Editor Stephen Adamson; Designer James Campus; Photographer: John Campbell; Illustrators: Jonathan Inglis, Aziz Khan. Typeset by Consort Art Graphics. Printed in Great Britain by Redwood Burn Ltd.

Martin Brown: tension at the Palladium

MARTIN BROWN MAKES IT BIG

Tuesday sees the start of another series of 'Out Of Your Depth' – the programme that gives some lucky person the chance to break into The Big Time, by throwing them 'in at the deep end' to see how far they sink

THIS WEEK it's the chance to hear how Martin Brown got chosen by Sir Norman Tonsil from a shortlist of one to try his hand at various jobs in the entertainment world in the hope that he eventually found one he could do successfully.

Acting

Day One, and Martin's first job as an actor is secured. And it's a part that's ideally suited to him – that of an extra who is spat on. There was one problem, however, because for his gruelling part Martin would be required to say one line. Hence his first visit to Dame Peggy Darling, now a drama teacher at the London Academy of Drama and Institute of Dramatic Art, or LADIDA as it's known. Dame Peggy began with voice training.

'Now a deep breath, Martin, and from the stomach, project!'

At first attempt, Martin completely misunderstood, and vomited all over Dame Peggy and her carpet. She decided to adopt a different approach.

'Just relax, then, Martin, let everything go loose. Now flex the tummy muscles and…'

What followed was of immense embarrassment to all those present, particularly Martin, who spent the rest of the lesson in a towel whilst his trousers dried off.

From then on Dame Peggy abandoned any exercises requiring muscle control of any sort, and concentrated on diction.

'Peter Piper picked a peck of peppers. Say it!'

Martin took a deep breath, drew himself up to his full height and emitted what can only be described as 'saliva'. Having now thrown up over her carpet, filled his trousers

**Out Of Your Depth
Wednesday 4.45**

in her presence, and gobbed in her eye, it was decided that Martin should thank Dame Peggy for her time and bid farewell to both her and the chance of ever becoming an actor.

Comedian

Day Two, and a new tack was needed. We looked for clues in his fan mail. Many of his listeners' letters seemed to mention a sense of humour:

'He seems to have no sense of humour,' *A. Barking, Leics.*

'I find him completely laughable,' *D. Totteridge, Notts.*

'Is Martin Brown some sort of joke?' *M. Malcolm, Sussex.*

So Martin, we felt, was clearly cut out to be a stand-up comic.

For the best advice possible we went to comedy scriptwriter, Dick Joy, the man responsible for such comedy classics as *Yours Aren't Big Enough, Not On My Wife* and *It Don't Half Stick out of My Trousers, Mum!*

Dick it was that set about teaching Martin to write his own 'gags' by giving him as a model: 'The other day I went to an Irish take-away – the only trouble was I got soup in a basket', and getting Martin to think up others like it. Here are some of the results of Martin's wit:

'The other day I went to an American take-away and I had a hamburger.'

'The other day I went to a Japanese take-away – the only trouble was I didn't like the food – it

was all rather too spicy and some of it wasn't even cooked.'

'The other day I went to a Swiss take-away – the only trouble was they were neutral in both World Wars.' © *Martin Brown*

Day Three, and armed with his jokes Martin was booked to appear at the London Palladium in front of 2500 people. Anna Daptor's on-the-spot interview with Martin just before he went on is an all-time classic piece of broadcasting, insofar as it showed the nervous tension backstage and it also prevented Martin from being ready in time for his introduction.

It's possible the London Palladium audience was not ready for the sight of a man shuffling on stage with his trousers round his ankles, clutching a toilet roll in one hand and his underpants in the other. But it did at least provide the first and indeed only laugh of the performance. Martin subsequently required hospital treatment, and it took a team of doctors over 3 hours to recover the microphone.

Lion-Tamer

Day Four. It was following the Palladium riot, that, on the insistence of Sir Norman himself, Martin tried his hand at lion-taming. He started gently with the lions inside the cage and Martin outside getting used to them.

Day Five. After one day, he moved on – with Martin inside and the lions outside getting used to him.

Day Six. And finally the big moment. Both Martin and the lions, together outside the cage, with Martin trying like hell to get back in again.

Mime Artist

Day Seven, and Martin's visit to a Mime School, which was run by an elderly, frail woman called Renata who grimaced oddly when Martin shook and apparently broke her hand as they were introduced. She began by telling the class to imagine they were flowers, which in Martin's case was not particularly difficult. This was further proven when they were asked to walk against the wind, as Martin suddenly fell to the floor and claimed his stalk had broken. It was then explained to him that these were two quite separate exercises and that he should put being a flower from his mind. At this point there was some heated discussion after which they agreed to differ, smiled warmly at each other, and Martin shook and broke her other hand.

The group was then asked to split into couples, and such was the impression Martin had already given that the rest of the group formed a circle in the middle of the room, and picked straws for who should be his partner. A grown man with a beard broke down and wept, and the straws had to be picked again. After two subsequent suicide attempts, the short straw was finally taken by a young lady in a leotard.

The couples were instructed to mimic each others' movements mirroring exactly whatever the other did. A maniacal leer came over Martin's face as he began wilfully to rip all his clothes off in the vain hope that his partner would do the same. The sight of Martin standing stark naked in the centre of the room, grinning expectantly at his bewildered partner, is one those present will never be able to erase from their memories. Furthermore, an unfortunate turn of phrase which Renata then chose to use, namely 'Hold everything', prompted Martin to indulge in a visual joke which amused neither the assembled company nor the judge who, the next day, sentenced him to two months' imprisonment for public self-abuse. ■

Martin Brown's new show can now be heard by tuning into Radio Pentonville (Tuesdays, 5 – 5.5 am).

Arts Olé!

A round-up of what's on in the world of the arts

What's Going On, 5.0 Daily

RADIO ACTIVE's regular contributors to the awards-losing arts programme were asked by the *Radio Active Times* to provide a round-up of what's on in the arts, which they conscientiously agreed to do.

Theatre

Sebastian Wally on The National Theatre's new production of *Hamlet.*

'Ah, well now. It's been a bit of a busy week, I'm afraid, and I didn't actually get to see it. Sorry about that.'

Exhibitions

Julian Bickerstaffe on the retrospective exhibition of Aubrey Bumpington's Stained Concrete work at the Roffredo Tortellini alla Panna Gallery (until November 23rd).

'It has just been impossible, I'm afraid, darling. I've been up to my eyes in decorating the new conservatory all week. I did it all green and then, disaster, it didn't go with the scatter cushions so I had to do the *whole* lot again in mauve. It has just been a nightmare and I'm afraid poor Aubrey's stained concrete just had to go out of the window.'

Books

Lady Anabelle Lever on Timothy Mo's unfinished new book *Half a Mo,* a new Greene, a new Green, and a previously unpublished Greenn.

'It has just been dinner parties all week, I'm afraid. I did start one of them, but the phone went and it was Tina and we got chatting about *that* do at the ffinch's the other week and you know how Tina goes on, especially when she gets on to the subject of *H.R.H. and the cocktail sausages* . . . so after that I was just in a *whirl* trying to catch up. But *do* send me some more books to look at next week; they help to fill up the empty shelf next to the *Monet.*'

Opera

Giles d'Ubious on Erkel's *Hunyadi Laszlo* (Opera North, Wiesbaden) and Hunyadi Laszlo's *Erkel* (Opera South, Baden-Baden-Pardon).

'Actually, I didn't see either of them, but I did see something else last week which I found moved and gripped me more than anything since P.Q.R.S.D. Bach's *Toccata and Fog in D.* The film *Bambi.*

To me it seemed to be a film which was, in many ways, about a little deer called Bambi and a rabbit called Thumper. I still find myself humming that haunting aria 'Drip, drip, drip little rain drops falling'. And the ensemble playing is superb.'

Television

Richard Inglenook on *Goodbye Mum,* a new BBC situation comedy starring Molly Sugden, and the moving documentary on euthanasia, *Goodbye Mum.*

'I don't have a television, I'm afraid. I've seen *Bambi,* though, if that's any help.'

A Word from God

ɩarm, and merriment and fulfil-
ɩent and felicity and exhilaration,
ɩd relish and indulgence and glee
ɩd frolic, and delectation and
ɩmusement and vivacity and spirit,
ɩd geniality and good humour and
ɩveliness and laughter; about gai-
y and folly and jocularity and
ɔod cheer, and vitality and joie de
ɩvre and sparkle and animation,
ɩd revel and abandon and smiling
ɩd comedy, and chuckling and
ɩortling and giggling and twinkle;
bout entertainment and diversion
ɩd recreation and solace, and
ɩlaxation and leisure and refresh-
ɩent and rejuvenation, and festiv-
y and jollification and foolery and
ɔree; about skylarking and capers
ɩd romping and pranks, and feast-
ɩg and revelling and carousing and
igh jinks; about diversion and in-

(cont. p.53)

A LOVIN' KINDA LOVIN'
The Dreary Wet Band
(Composed by The Dreary Wet Band,
Ponce and Sir Norman Tonsil)
STEREOTYPE SOUND

Radio Active Records

ɩe hugely popular Radio Active
ɩbel was the brainchild of Sir
ɩorman Tonsil, who realised that
y starting our own company we
ɔuld provide a uniquely direct link
ɩetween the product and the dist-
ɩbutor, maximise the efficiency of
ɩe station, and make ourselves an
ɩormous amount of boodle. The
ɩbel is a marvellous outlet for new
ɩlent: the cost of signing a new
ɩoup requires only a modest outlay
f about £10,000, and we find that
ɩost managers are only too willing
ɔ cough up those sorts of shekels in
ɩturn for a guarantee of saturation
ir play. ∎

The true story of the Second World War

He's tough. He's deadly

He rescues the troops at Dunkirk

He defeats Rommel in Egypt

He overcomes Hitler in a spectacular car chase . . .

And ALL without a single line of intelligible dialogue

SYLVESTER STALLONE
is the entire British and American armies in

THE INVADER

Also starring CHUCK NORRIS as Field Marshall Montgomery   ARNOLD SCHWARTZENEGER as Vera Lynn

The story as it's never been believed before!

Is nuclear war a good thing or what?

This week's Mass Debate, live from the Radio Active foyer, concentrates on the burning issue of nuclear war, as it debates the motion, 'This house is in favour of all-out nuclear war and the destruction of the earth as we know it'

Temporary home for the Cabinet
High risk of death
50% mortality
60% mortality
Overcast conditions for a few months
Avoid lamb chops
Nuclear winter
Misguided Cruise missiles
Epicentre
Sunglasses advisable
General: Hard rain in all area

Radio Active's Mass Debate, Sunday 10.0

AS a forerunner to Monday's debate, Radio Active last week broadcast a radio version of *Threads* – the chilling dramatisation of what would happen if a nuclear bomb dropped on Britain. Its effect on the Radio Active listeners was tremendous and letters have been pouring in:

'I enjoyed it a great deal, but why did it have to have such a sad ending?'
Steven Cordingley, Bucks.

'A most entertaining programme. Could you please tell me what the signature tune was?' *Sandra Ashcroft*, Little Tewksbury

'Frankly I found it very noisy. And whatever happened to the weather forecast at 2 minutes past?'
Wilfred Robertson, Edinburgh

'For the most part, an extremely good dramatisation, but surely it should be "none of these *is* edible" and not "none of these *are* edible"?'
Dr. Bernard Plumpton, Wilts.

So obviously the point got home forcefully with the Radio Active listeners at home.

This Week's Panel

But what about our panellists for this week's debate? How do they view the threat of nuclear war and do they think nuclear weapons act as a deterrent?

Reverend John Whitfield, Archdeacon of Uckfield:

'I remember my first wife, Françoise, used to ask me if I thought nuclear weapons acted as a detergent! And the first time she heard the expression nuclear disarmament, she thought it was an advertisement for "New Clear Disarma Mints"! But that's plainly stupid. As indeed she was as I recall.'

Douglas Polting, Conservative MP for Frognal, Minister for Keeping Everything Nice and Happy:

'You know, there's an awful lot of gloom and doom talked about the bomb dropping, but you've got to look on the bright side. For a start, there will be a temporary amnesty on library fines, and in the event of a holocaust, municipal swimming pools will be completely free to the public.'

General Anthony Corpse, of Her Majesty's Royal Straight-Jackets:

'The thing is, you can't say you wouldn't want to be bombed in a nuclear attack, if you've never been bombed. You might quite like it. Lots of chaps in the last war quite took to it. Said it gave them a chance to see just what sort of stuff they were made of.'

Joan Tilley, spokesperson for CND and active pacifist:

'In the event of a nuclear attack, CND recommend that you have about your person some sort of protective headgear, such as an inverted colander or a skateboard, which you should then attach to your head with glue or string, as holding on to it will mean your hands come off worse, in the case of a direct hit.'

Spontaneous Combustion

So what exactly would happen to the British Isles if a 50 megaton bomb were dropped on Trafalgar Square? Radio Active Weatherman, **Dick Barnes,** gave us his views:

'As you'd expect Central London will get the worst of it. Total obliteration there, with the possibility of a raging inferno. Further out, around the outskirts of Greater London, milder holocaust, but still with total annihilation and death within 6 minutes. Out in the Home Counties, you can expect some pretty high temperatures, somewhere around 800 or 900 degrees Celsius, with the prospect of some widespread spontaneous comb tion.

'Further out still, up in Midlands, East Anglia, Sou Coast and most of the W Country, wintry conditic for some 20 or 30 years, w the sun rays unable really penetrate the nuclear clc at all – so wrap up well, wo you?

'Have a nice weekend!'

Life

Naturally, a nuclear atta would affect all aspects contemporary life, and *Ra Active* is particularly c cerned with its effect on t music scene and the char Top DJ **Mike Flex** will presenting his view on t week's show. 'Obviously t charts won't be coming every week. But *Melo Maker* say they hope continue with a monthly T Ten based on what people humming in the street.

'Also, the bomb would bri about an end to most of t wimpy synthesizer bands a a return to acoustic inst ments. Possibly heavy rc would make a comeback, althou people finding a lot of hea rocks about the place a starting to bang them togeth And it would probably me an end to the video boo with the emphasis returni to live performances, althou it's unlikely that large crow would turn out just to he people banging rocks.' ∎

Win your very own

RADIO ACTIVE

Fall-out Shelter

This fabulous fall-out shelter can be yours
Can be erected within the four minute
warning, as long as you don't hit your
thumbs while hammering in the pegs
Guaranteed against fireballs, nuclear
radiation, thermal heat, ground shock,
air blast, nuclear fall-out and theft*

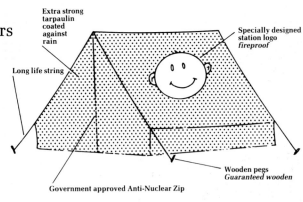

Extra strong
tarpaulin
coated
against
rain

Specially designed
station logo
fireproof

Long life string

Government approved Anti-Nuclear Zip

Wooden pegs
Guaranteed wooden

And this can be yours
absolutely free if you win
our competition
All you have to do
is put the funniest face
on Mr Mushroom Cloud
Here's our example,
we're sure you can do
better than that!

'IT may be Radio Active,
but it's certainly *not* radio-active!'

*PROBABLY

SATURDAY

RA
MW 92·59
+87·4m
581 kHz
until
2.0pm

Thereafter 390m 740 kHz long wave in mono + vice-versa

All programme times liable to alteration in the event of Martin Brown's News round-up overrunning by more than an hour

5.30 am Wey, Hey, It's Saturday!!

Yes, it's Saturday, it's five-thirty in the morning, and that means it's time for you kiddies to get out of bed and wake up your parents. Today we attempt to break the all-time world record for a train journey from Paddington to Tewkesbury! **Uncle Mike Stand** will be in the Comfy Corner, **Martin Brown** will be in the Romper Room, and **Mike Channel** will be saying 'Ark, Ark' as Aaron the Aardvark in the outside Coal Bunker. And we try and solve some of the problems concerned with glue-sniffing – how to make sure you're not ripped off, where to buy it in bulk and how to squeeze the last little bits left in the bottom.

10.0 Meet Your Idol

This week **Jimmy Saville,** talking to JIMMY SAVILLE.

11.0 Good Day Sport

(Timings are subject to being arbitrarily changed if anything more interesting turns up)

11.05 Indoor Hang-Gliding from Bristol

11.45 Long-Distance Gardening

12.00 Competitive 5-A-Side Sleeping from Brighton

12.45 The Olympic Games

12.48 Welterweight and Heavyweight Ice Skating

2.00 Boxing, Hurling, Diving, Wrestling and Shooting – The Football International between Uruguay and Italy

As a special service for the hard of hearing tune to 9438 kHz Medium Wave, where all Radio Active programmes are shouted.

Radio Active's own stars of the court warm up for SW17
11.0 am Good Day Sport

3.00 Wimbledon Tennis Championships

Live and exclusive coverage of *Radio Active's* tennis tournament on South Wimbledon's prestigious Recreation Ground.

Uncle Mike Stand provides ball-by-ball commentary as the balls come out of their boxes, **Nigel Pry** discusses base-line rallies and psychological preparation with the umpire's chair, and **Martin Brown** mingles with the strawberries. Plus expert comments from self-styled friend to all the stars, **Gerald Brownnoser,** and the man they call Mr Wimbledon – **Dan Wimbledon.**
Stereo

4.45 Classified Football Results

Accompanied by background music from the JESUS AND MARY CHAIN and read by the bass-guitarist of THE HOUSEMARTINS.
Mono with occasional Stereo

5.0 Weather Report

Cloudy with occasional Showers
(Broadcast 27 February)

5.5 Afternoon Theatre

A sensitive look at one man's psychiatric problems and how he comes to terms with it, in **Hey, Look At Me, I'm Bonkers,** by SIMON SQUATT.

6.15 Uncle Mike'll Fix It

This week **Uncle Mike** fixes it for an eight-year-old schoolboy to spend three weeks in a Paris brothel.

7.30 Pick of the Continuity Announcements

Some of the best of last week's continuity announcements, including *Here is the News, That was the News,* and *Oh my God, I've come in in the middle of the News by mistake.* Also a selection from the 500 impersonations of farmyard animals performed by our continuity announcer last Tuesday after Nigel Pry failed to turn up for his show.

8.45 Do Your Own Thing

This week's DIY show tells you how to make a bedside lamp out of just a piece of wire, a light bulb and a lampshade, and how to make an omelette with just three eggs, a frying pan and some heat, and there will be the final set of instructions for all those of you making the Geiger counter out of two milk bottle tops and a toilet roll.

10.0 Did You Catch It?

A look back over the week's broadcasting with **Sir Norman Tonsil,** who this week is joined by **John Salmon,** actor with the Royal Shakespeare Company and currently appearing in *Sooty's Magic Wonder Show,* **Jill Mason,** editor of the new women's magazine *Tampon,* and **Anthony Shane,** author, raconteur and devout homosexual.

11.0 The Toilet Programme

The Bishop of Luton talks to **Martin Brown** about books he likes to read on the toilet.

4.0 am *VHF only* Minorities Programme

In order to keep its franchise *Radio Active* is providing half-an-hour of this peak-time slot, normally occupied by Mike Channel, to all the minority groups in the country and extends a warm and welcoming hand to every religious crank, sexual deviant, candidate for the funny farm, one-armed pigeon fancier and Welshman, who wants to get his point of view across.
(Subject to cancellation if the tennis is overrunning)

4.30 You, The Night and A Bottle of Mogadon

Presented by **Mike Channel.** Listeners to Mike's old peak-time mid-morning show can now catch him at the slightly earlier time of 4 am. An easy listening show for all insomniacs.

COMMUNITY SERVICE

Radio Active does a good deal of 'behind the scenes' work for and on behalf of 'the community'; something we seldom shout about on the station although it is widely advertised in all the national Press. Our community telephone lines are open at all times (weekends and evenings excepted). These include the *I'm in Trouble* line, a friendly service for general help and guidance, the *Oh God, I'm Unemployed* line, which provides help for the jobless, the *Shit a Brick I've Got Nowhere to Live* line, for flathunters and hippies, and our *Christ Almighty, I'm Starving to Death Here and You Bastards Don't Seem to be Able to Do Anything About It* line.

The Right Reverend Reverend Wright writes: 'I don't know if you have ever considered ringing up a radio station to discuss your personal problems, because I'm not a mind-reader, so there's no way I could know – but if you have then you could do a lot worse than phone one of the Radio Active community lines. You could shoot a defenceless dog or drive a stake through the heart of a close friend, for example, both of which would be worse. But if you have no desire to do either of these things, then why not give us a call? Well, perhaps your phone's out of order or maybe you'd planned to water the rubber plant, or clean the inside of your kettle – there are any number of reasons why you might not be able to ring us, now I come to think of it.'

SUNDAY

6 am Radio Active's Radiothon

Fun, fun, fun. A chance to have the time of your life giving away all of your money.

6 pm Closedown

RA BMW 1600
VW 1300
+
Sinclair
C5
27.5

Broadcasting on the same wave-length as all the local taxis.

8.0 am Bedrock

Mike Flex's Breakfast-Show
Mike Flex takes over Mike Channel's old show and brings you a brand new sound, including traffic reports, time-checks, music, time-checks, the usual competitions and phone-ins, time-checks and a host of other great new features, including time-checks.

1.0 pm Anna Daptor's Lunchtime Show

Anna keeps you company whatever you're doing – whether you're in the office, in your car, still at home, or just sleeping with some of your husband's golfing friends. Plus at 2.0 *Anna's Gourmet Meal Recipe (see apology).*

APOLOGY

Anna Daptor would like to apologise for some slight errors contained in last week's Gourmet Meal Recipe.

Firstly, unfortunately no mention was made that the turkey should have been cooked.

Secondly, the oven temperature should have been Gas Mark 3, and not Gas Mark 30 as Anna said. She would like to apologise to all those people who were unable to get close enough to their ovens to turn them off.

Thirdly, while Anna did say that you could use most types of oil in the salad dressing she should perhaps not have specifically recommended Castrol GTX. Particular apologies to Mrs Henderson of Frome who apparently drained it out of her car engine and was unable to get her car started to take herself to the hospital.

You may be interested to know that a book is available called *Anna's Gourmet Recipes,* price £2.95, which you can obtain from Radio Active together with its companion volume *Anna's Gourmet Recipe Amendments,* price £15.95.

Mike Channel presents the award to the winner of his look-alike competition
4.30 am, You, The Night and A Bottle of Mogadon

3.30 Nigel Pry Show

'Yes, again me Nigel for an hour or four or half, my show the happy sounds of music, competitions, and literally reports from here and all around, tune in why not?'
Once again Nigel attempts to get more than 45 seconds into his show without electrocuting himself.

*CEEFAX SUBTITLES

4.0 At Last It's Christmas!

Almost 1986 years ago a little baby boy was born in Bethlehem, and to mark that occasion *Radio Active* will be linking up with **Radio Bethlehem. Uncle Mike Stand** spends Christmas day in the company of some small children and is remanded in custody in the evening.
(Broadcast 26 June this year)

5.0 What's Going On

Our daily look at what's happening locally across the nation, with **Anna Daptor** and **Sir Norman Tonsil.** Art, theatre education, literature, canoeing and music, with special guests popping in to tell you where to go.

6.0 Amateur DJ Competition

Our competition to find the best amateur DJ around. And for those who look like being a *Star in the Making,* a special nine-year contract with Radio Reykjavik.

7.0 The Golden Oldies Show

Martin Brown plays all the hits from one year. Today it's 1873, so that's a must for all Cliff Richard fans.

8.0 Elvis Presley – Live in Concert

Lovely old dead Elvis in a concert he recorded while he was still alive.

10.30 The Bio Show

Actor **Sir John Leslie** tells us about his life in the theatre from his first big break in the chorus of Ralph Reader's Gang Show to where he is today – doing voice-overs for margarine commercials. We reunite Sir John with some old chums: actor-manager **Sir Donald Stuffy,** who gave him much invaluable advice such as 'Never go on the stage', Italian film director **Fellanti,** who fondly remembers him as *'bastardo',* and **Dame Gloria Thornpickle,** who remembers him as 'that cocky little shit'.

11.58 A Look Askance

Anthony Strumpkins takes a whimsical but irreverent gallop through the sound archives and comes back with his trousers round his ankles.

1.00 am Midnight Theatre

'Feminists Against Radio' with a new production of BERTOLT BRECHT'S classic masterpiece, *Der Muttervöker von Köln* (The Incestuous Person of Cologne), which the group will refuse to perform at one o'clock this morning.

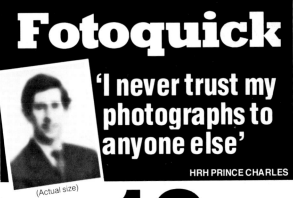

RA

**64.5F
18.2C
SUNNY** WITH
**OCCASIONAL
SHOWERS**

Max. 22C (72F) (MW only)

5.0 am Hello Indians

Mike Channel has great pleasure in presenting this early early-morning show in Urdu.

8.0 Bedrock

Mike Flex with better news, fuller weather reports, and fatter and camper astrologers than any other breakfast show. Amongst today's requests Mike will be playing 'I'd Rather Go Blind' for patients at the Institute for the Hard-of-Hearing, 'When I'm Dead and Gone' for an elderly pensioner suffering from depression, and Clodagh Rogers singing 'Jack in a Box' for a lady whose husband has just passed away.

1.0 pm Anna Daptor's Lunchtime Show

Live from the **Stamford Townswomen's Guild Flower Show** (All proceeds to the Palestine Liberation Front). Her special guest today, the **Bishop of Swindon**, will be there to help her pick out the Bingo cards. Plus some unusual country recipes from local culinary expert and wife to a farmer to boot, **Mrs Janet Toboot**, including Slug Vongole and Escalope of Vole.

APOLOGY

Radio Active's Traffic Department would like to apologise for an incorrect announcement made during last Thursday's 'Eleven O'Clock Show', which was due to a slight typing error. The message should have read, *'Due to industrial action, there'll be no buses running tomorrow morning in the city centre'*, and not as was announced, *'Due to industrial action, there'll be no busy ranging tomaxjiff in die caty sintrad.'*

3.0 Fun Day

Radio Active's jocks go out and about on our Fun Day! Coming live from the fun fair at **Blackport**, and featuring *Guess the Age of the Big Dipper, Guess the Weight of Anna Daptor,* and *Pin a Tail on Julie Andrews.* Plus Uncle Mike Stand's *'Guess What This Object Is'* competition: once again **Uncle Mike** will be showing an object to kids around the fair and hoping to keep out of the way of the local constabulary. Our sponsors, *Cadaver Cigarettes,* have generously donated 1,000 free packets to be given away, so that should really keep the kiddies hooked.

Outside Broadcast

TOMBOLA PRIZES!

Winners of last month's Tombola prizes at the Radio Active Fun Day were as follows:
3rd Prize Bottle of Nina Ricci perfume and make-up kit.
Winner: **Arnold Hughes** of Biggleswade
2nd Prize Philips sun-ray lamp and sun-bed.
Winner: **Mr and Mrs Ismael** and **Esmir Biryani** of Hatfield
1st Prize Crate of Glenfiddich whisky
Winner: **Simon Davis** of Cheltenham, aged 7

Anna snatches a light snack between the courses of her lunchtime recipes
1.0 pm Anna Daptor's Lunchtime Show

5.30 Radio Active Playhouse

This week the rolling hills of the Scottish Highlands with the purple heather and deep blue lochs are far from our thoughts as we are transported back to the Chicago of the 1920s. The play *Of Dirty Mice* begins near the start of Act One and tells of the assassination of gang leader Joe Gazpacho.
(Broadcast 7 February 9.19 pm)
'A dramatised stench' *The Guardian*
'Let's hope they don't repeat this one in a hurry' *The Listener*

Inside Broadcast

6.30 Best of the Week

Extracts from some of the best moments of last week's broadcasting. It was such a good week that today's show lasts a full hour rather than the usual 90 minutes.

Stereo with mono

7.0 Good Morning Monday

Our bubbling chat show that gets your week off to a sunny start.

Mono (Broadcast slightly later than usual)

8.15 In Concert

The Alarm — Recorded at the Hammersmith Odeon. Unfortunately they were playing the National Exhibition Centre in Birmingham at the time.

1/2 Track Mono

10.0 God Alone Knows

Our Sunday morning religious programme, broadcast as ever on Tuesday evening. **The Right Reverend Reverend Wright** brings you the top ten commandments as voted by you the *Radio Active* listeners. There'll be the usual hymns, prayers, and dedications, and the lines to God will be open from 10.15.
Megaphone

11.0 Book Now!

Sebastian Wally looks at an extract from *Samantha's Passage* a new novel by Suzanne Jacks, shortly to be remaindered, and examines the increasingly worrying problem of adullt ilitracey. Plus a review of Douglas Kempton's marvellously detailed series of autobiographies: *As I Got Up One Morning, As I Went Downstairs To Get the Papers, As I Went To the Toilet,* and his latest, *As I Sat There Waiting For the Movements To Start.*

WEDNESDAY

Today Radio Active is 19 years old!
And to celebrate that fact all the Radio Active disc-jockeys will be out and about, getting very pissed. So there'll be no programmes broadcast until Thursday morning.

Owing to a misunderstanding at the printer's, all Thursday's programmes are shown elsewhere in the magazine as being transmitted at 11am. In order therefore not to disappoint those listeners who will be tuning in to hear their favourite shows at that time, *Radio Active* will now be broadcasting all the day's programmes simultaneously then.

FRIDAY

| 400m LW |
| 200m MW |
| 100m hurdles |
| VHF |

Programmes are in stereo, except where indicated(*)

7.0 am* News

7.1* News Stories behind the Headlines

7.3* News Story about a Pet in Your Local Area Doing Something Endearing

7.14* The Main Points Again

7.15* Nigel Pry

Nigel Pry presents some of his favourite music with the help of his special guest, **Mike Flex.**

8.00* Bedrock

Mike Flex plays some of his favourite music with the help of his special guest, **Nigel Pry.** Also the new *Radio Active* 'Record of the Week' released on the new *Radio Active* label and played on *Radio Active* every quarter of an hour until it gets into the charts.

8.15* Top Ten Teasers

Do you want to make a lot of money with the minimum of effort? Tune in to Mike Flex for his 'Top Ten Teasers' and see how it's done.

1.0 pm* Anna Daptor's Lunchtime Show

Weight Watchers Special. How to eat lots of food – then sit back and watch yourself put on weight. Plus a few more recipes to help clear out the larder: today's specials – Gratin of Winkles and Pickled Cucumbers à la Treacle. Anna also tells you how to plan a dinner party, starting with French Onion Soup (*MW only; LW: Casserole and Dumplings, except LW in the North of England, who join SW listeners for* Buttered Carrots. *On VHF:* Puddings).

3.0* Martin Brown Show

All Martin's usual features including *Lose the Record, Find the Record Again*, and *Put the Record on at the Wrong Speed.* Plus a special Celebrity Interview. Martin will be talking to Bruce Springsteen, asking him when he first took up the trumpet, whether he'd like a biscuit and who he is, while Bruce will be asking Martin how he managed to get this job.

5.0* What's Going On

Today *Radio Active's* look at the Arts concentrates on the Prison Theatre Company, the cast of which are all out on parole to perform their show *Live At Her Majesty's Pleasure.* On its opening night it had a cast of over 50, but within a week it had shrunk to 3, all of them handcuffed to uniformed police officers. **Sebastian Wally** reports.

5.55* Choir of the Year

Sebastian stays on to look back on this week's final of our *Choir of the Year* Competition, and asks whether it was a good idea to decide it by a tug-of-war.

6.30* Round Your Parts

Anna Daptor visits the rural villages of Humpingham, Strokingham, Lickenham and Wallop. She chats with the locals, gets to know them and decides whether they are the most difficult, moronic and generally retarded people she has ever had the misfortune of meeting.

7.0* In Concert

Bob Morley and the Wailers British light comedy actor **Robert Morley** shows another side of his personality as he brings us three hours of Reggae from the **Marquee** in London.

8.0* Backchat

A chance for listeners to air their views on the station's output. Tonight allegations of political bias in our current affairs programmes, to be answered in full by *Radio Active's* Head of Carpets.

9.0* Organ Up

Oivind Vinstra plays your requests for music on the mouth organ.

10.0* Weather

A look at today's weather for anyone who missed it.

10.5* Weather Forecast

A look at tomorrow's weather.

Bob Morley and the Wailers
7.0 In Concert

10.10* Problem Phone-in

Lady Cecily Fenton helps you with your personal, emotional and amorous problems. Even members of the lower classes are welcome to phone in, and Lady Cecily will be delighted to talk to them about how things are down there.

10.30* Hunt Stunts

Another outing with 'Oh so daring' **Mike Hunt,** the man who has fought a bull in a Spanish bull-ring and killed it with the aid of only a .22 Magnum and who has escaped from Hampton Court Maze in just 7 minutes with nothing but a high-powered chain-saw. Today he reports on the success of this year's adventure holiday which gave 25 deprived East End kids the opportunity re-create the journey of one of Britain's most famous explorers, in Operation Scott. Equipped with only *Radio Active* T-shirts and a packet of sandwiches (provided free by the station) these kids, many of whom didn't have a pair of shoes to their name, faithfully followed Captain Scott's expedition right through to the end.

11.30* Obituary: Mike Channel

Mike Flex presents a portrait of the 'Doddery Old Man of the Airwaves' whose sad and unseemly death over a primus stove in the kitchen of his Bermondsey bed-sit occurred in the early hours of this morning. Mike pays tribute to the man who was quite well-respected within the profession and much liked by a reasonable number of listeners, and takes consolation from the fact that his death occurred at a time when his career was in any case so very nearly at an end.
(Programme subject to Mike Channel dying overnight.)

NEXT WEEK

Next Sunday *Radio Active* will split frequencies for the very first time. Listeners on FM can hear a lot of **Dire Straits** records played on compact disc, whilst listeners under the age of 45 on AM will hear their usual programmes introduced by a lot of disc-jockeys disgruntled because their audiences have been cut in half.

Who to top Radio Active Music Festival

As yet the top act has not been booked, so the question 'Who is to top the Radio Active Music Festival?' remains

Music Festival Wednesday, All Day

The Radio Active Music Festival is fast becoming one of the most noteworthy events of the year. Already almost all the local police stations have it ringed in their calendars, and every extremist pressure-group in the country will be hoping for a repeat of last year's riotous entertainment.

PLUS this year we hope to have some music . . .

And for those who aren't into Rock, there's a special jazz concert live from the *Toad and Scrotum* in Tooting, given by 'de Man wi' de Rhythm', as he's known on the pub circuit in South London, Hoagey Dobson.

A brief glimpse of this letter from our sponsors, Wallocks Real Ales, will give you some idea of the star-studded line-up we aim to bring you.

Along with the great names of pop, the Festival will play host to some up-and-coming bands like *Y. Y. Wicket*, *Trouser Experience*, *Hatfield Peverel* and *Sprunt*.

Hoagey Dobson sings

Boogie-woogie Bugle Boy from East Croydon

String of Purleys

By the Time I Get To Finchley

Do You Know The Way To Sevenoaks?

Blue Ridge Mountains of New Malden

Yellow Rose of Bagshot

Mogador 65000

Is It True What They Say About Bromley?

Gillingham On My Mind

What Made Millwall Quay Famous

Hoagey: goes gold

Sprunt, whose negro-spiritual and jazz-funk influences combine with techno-electronic synthesised rhythm sections in 9/8 time on their latest single Suck This!

MIKE FLEX'S HISTORY OF ROCK

INCLUDED in this year's Music Festival is Mike Flex's celebrated *History Of Rock*, an in-depth survey of rock music over the last 30 years, with one of the biggest programme budgets in the history of *Radio Active*.

Sydney *Mike tries out some Oysters Kilpatrick whilst catching up with London-based sound engineer Bill Symmonds, responsible for recording some of today's best-known Kelloggs jingles.*

L.A. *Mike joins Tom Henderson, former record shop-owner, who recalls some of the highlights of his life over a couple of Lobster Thermidor and some Chablis.*

Memphis *Mike chats with record producer Greg Amos over lunch.*

Barbados *Mike has an after-dinner chat with Wigan estate-agent Tim Jarvis about their favourite Beatles records.*

AND as a climax to the Festival, the Radio Active Drama Repertory Company have agreed to perform in its entirety their new musical written and directed by themselves, and based on the life and times of King Harold, entitled *One In The Eye.*

I

HAROLD: You are my love, you are my only own
   From your head right down to your knucklebone
   I'd willingly give up my throne
   For one smell of your lovely eau de Cologne

   Oh heavens, by Jove
QUEEN: Now we're in love
HAROLD: I'll wear your hose
QUEEN: I'll be your spouse
HAROLD: Till death us do part
QUEEN: We won't be half heart-
BOTH: -Ed about it!

II

BOTH: H-A-A-A-A-A-A-ASTINGS!
   Where the wind comes whipping off the sea
   That is where we'll fight
   From dawn till night
   And some of us will be wounded and others will probably
   Die rather horribly
   But we're prepared to pay the price
   We're all prepared to make a sac-
   Rifice!

III

QUEEN: Goodbye, goodbye, my Anglo-Saxon guy
   Try not to get an arrow in your eye!

In today's fast moving world it's good to know that there's still somebody who doesn't care about always having to get somewhere on time

BRITISH RAIL

If you are going away
on holiday . . .

DO
Lock your windows

Close your doors

Let a neighbour know
that you're going away

ANOTHER PARALYSINGLY OBVIOUS PUBLIC INFORMATION ANNOUNCEMENT

DJ
TEST

RADIO OXFORD
AND CAMBRIDGE
BOARD

Three Hours
Candidates are required
to take four commercial
breaks an hour.

Satin bomber jackets must be worn at all times. Candidates are asked to write on the paper. If they are unable to write they should dictate their answers in the box provided.

SURNAME ....INITIALS...................

1. You accidentally put a record on at the wrong speed. Do you:

   A. Gradually creep it up to the right speed?
   B. Do the whole programme at half speed in the hope that people will just think there is something wrong with their radio?

2. In the middle of your show you are handed a piece of paper saying that Googie Withers has just died. Do you:

   A. Immediately dedicate a record to Googie Withers 'whoever she is, who died just a few minutes ago. So it's a big, big bye bye to her'?
   B. Ask the listeners to guess who has just died and say that whoever wins the competition will receive an album of her greatest hits?

3. The record player blows up. Do you:

   A. Fail to notice and keep trying to play records on it?
   B. Say, 'I'm sorry the record player has just broken, so in the meantime, while we're trying to mend it, here's a record'?

4. You're doing the early morning show and you're worried about oversleeping. Do you:

   A. Book an alarm call and then take the telephone off the hook when you go to bed?
   B. Try and stay awake all night and pass out at four o'clock in the morning in a seedy nightclub in Hartlepool?

5. You accidentally read out a request for a Lena Zavaroni record. Do you:

   A. Pretend you misread it and give the recipe for Zabaglioni?
   B. Play the record and leave your fader up while you make libellous remarks about her coming second to Marti Caine in an eating contest?

6. You are asked to read a news bulletin that is full of stories of death and disaster. Do you:

   A. Make up a story about a dog which has adopted a chicken and lead on that?
   B. Lighten the tone by doing a countdown of the top ten wars as researched by Gallup?

[Please flip over]

FINAL EDITION

DAILY BALLS

Tuesday August 5 1986   18p   ★★★★   THE VOICE OF BRITAIN

SOCCER HIGHLIGHTS A STRIKING PROBLEM PLUS · CRICKET SCORES · NIGHT RACING ... DOGS

UNITED THEY STAND!

BALLS OPINION: SEE PAGE 8

MANCHESTER UNITED 0, WEST HAM 0

A CLEAN and sporting match, marred only by the cynical murder of Cottee ten minutes in. It's only a shame that the referee wasn't in a good position to see it. In the 27th minute, a diving header from Norman Whiteside met Alvin Martin full in the stomach.

Shortly afterwards Mark Ward's head connected with Gordon Strachan's 31st minute fist and a quick exchange of moves left both players on the floor. Then in the 44th minute, a superb knee in the goolies from Frank McAvennie left Peter Davenport without any support up front. In the

second half, Robson played on r fully despite the loss of his arm tackle with Paris. Unfortunately, referee was not in a good positio see it, but shortly afterwards referee was thumped between the by Whiteside, and he was perfe positioned to see that.

BOXING'S BIG DECISION DAY

SCOTTISH Welterweight champion Jim Thugg lost his fight to retain his title against American Jeff Davies, here in Acapulco last night (writes Mike Cable backwards). Jim sustained an eye injury in the second round, but apparently insisted on carrying on. He received a broken nose in the 4th, but again resolved to continue. He was finally pursuaded to pull out at the end of the 7th round, after his head had been severed from his body. Jim's manager is confident, however, that Jim will be fit enough for next week's big fight in

No Goals in 0-0 Draw

ARSENAL 0, EVERTON 0

A GAME of two halves, with both teams playing 90 minutes and every player on the pitch play-ing football. With Arsenal kicking one way, and Everton kicking the other, it was clear we were in for a match in which neither side would

see that Arsenal had intention of shooting their own goalkeeper a Everton were in mu the same frame of mi at the other end. In fa neither side did get a g and to be frank, in t end, that was a f reflection of the sco

WIN £1m ON THE POOLS

VILLA AND C
IN FOOTBALL
MATCH

ASTON VILLA 5, MANCHESTER CITY 3

HOW well Villa must realise now that had they scored two goals fewer, they would have drawn this match. That's the harsh reality of football these days, where 5 minus 2 makes 3, and 3-all means a draw.

But that's not to take anything away from Aston Villa. They got 5 goals in the back of the net and that's good enough for a win when the other side only get three. City had two good chances to score late on, which would have meant a 5-all draw, and yet they could have missed the three they did get, which would have meant losing by an even greater margin, namely 5-0. But as it was they didn't.

DRAMATIC & IRRELEVANT HEADLINE

THROUGHOUT this match Molby in midfield for Liverpool was like a rock — solid and determined.

While Walsh was an absolute tiger up front — powerful, graceful, but always ready to strike unexpectedly. In the Forest defence, Metgod was a tower of strength — tall, firm as granite, resisting every tackle — while Sutton in goal stretching for everything, was like a piece of elastic. Up front, Franz Carr ran like a terrier — four lightly stumpy legs and a little wet nose. Beglin was for me a large green insect, while Whelan was a giant carrot in a top hat. I was on my feet shouting in the 53rd minute when the pitch turned into an enormous tidal wave and washed away the East Stand, but the match really ended for me 10 minutes from time, when I was taken out of the stadium by two men in white coats.

TODAY'S RACING — PAGES 26-27

Flower Arranging

DOROTHY JONES of Great Britain ran out overall winner in the International Flower Arranging at Crystal Palace yesterday afternoon. With only seconds remaining, and with the roses well to the left of the daffodils, Dorothy put in a late sprig to defeat the world champion, 18-stone Svetlana Vinovich. It wasn't elegant — I saw one or two roses upside down in the vase — but it seemed nothing was going to stop her. Pushing the chrysanthemums down with one fist, she grabbed a late handful of japonicas in all and a hollyhock before the

IN the Gymnastics contest yesterday between Great Britain, U.S.S.R., and Czechoslovakia, 17 year old Eva Petzjedrovchevic, a Glaswegian schoolgirl, scored maximum points in the final floor exercise, to give Great Britain a narrow victory, after the teams had been neck and neck all afternoon.

She began with a forward handspring, a double summersault, and an arab spring, going into a triple flic-flac, a fly-pigeon, a tummy turn, two belly flaps, a widgey wop, a backward turtle-bip, a front clip bodgey-twist, a firk, a fladge and finally a squadgey curdle-chop.

An X-certificate video of this has been rush-released by Warner Bros.

REST of SPORT IN SHORT

FOOTBALL

● Cliff Atkin, the £2 million West Bromwich Albion striker, has been put on the transfer list only hours after joining them from Arsenal with whom he spent just a day and a half. That was after spending the weekend as a Nottingham Forest player, and before that enjoying a very pleasant evening on the books of Leicester City, whom he joined from Tottenham Hotspur for whom he had signed that morning. Cliff, who receives 10 per cent of all transfer fees, is now a multi-millionaire at the age of 19, and intends retiring from league football without having played any.

● In last night's Second Division battle, Leeds United beat Crystal Palace 3-1. The scorer of all three Leeds goals was Jim Jackson, and all within the first 7 minutes. Jim was however able to get one back for his own side, before being substituted after quarter of an hour.

VIOLENT FANS

● Brighton Police have announced that because of the match tonight there'll be no public transport within 12 miles of the city centre, and they advise people to avoid the area as they expect violence from marauding fans. For those with tickets for the game, the bully-off has been changed to 7.30pm, and Roedean will be playing in yellow.

Fashion, Travel, Arts, Bingo—It's all been ditched to make way for Sport, Sport and even more Sport!

Are YOU lonesome tonight?

No need to be!
With computa-data

Yes, thousands of lonely hearts have become satisfied members, with COMPUTA-DATA. Just fill in our questionnaire and send it to us, and we will send you details of your ideal partner in absolute confidence in one of our gaily-coloured Computa-Data envelopes!

Helen and Graham—just one of the many brought together by Computa-Data

YOUR PERSONALITY
Are You

- ☐ Shy
- ☐ Nervous
- ☐ Affectionate
- ☐ Romantic
- ☐ Organised
- ☐ Outgoing
- ☐ Energetic
- ☐ Tidy
- ☐ Perverted
- ☐ Self-Confident

YOUR PARTNER
What do you look for in a perfect partner?

- ☐ Wit
- ☐ Charm
- ☐ Warmth
- ☐ Compassion
- ☐ Style
- ☐ Tolerance
- ☐ Excitement
- ☐ Long Tongue
- ☐ Generosity
- ☐ Understanding

YOUR INTERESTS
Tick any of the following you enjoy.

- ☐ Pop Music
- ☐ Dancing
- ☐ Cinema/Theatre
- ☐ Gardening
- ☐ Eating Own Excrement
- ☐ Travel
- ☐ Dining Out
- ☐ Museums
- ☐ Sport
- ☐ Poetry

WHAT AGE SHOULD YOUR PARTNER BE?

- ☐ 15-20   ☐ 40-50
- ☐ 20-30   ☐ 50 + over
- ☐ 30-40   ☐ Dead

HOW WOULD YOUR IDEAL PARTNER BE DRESSED?

- ☐ Smart   ☐ Nazi
- ☐ Modern   ☐ Scruffy
- ☐ Casual   ☐ Formal

WHICH OF THE FOLLOWING DO YOU FIND MOST ATTRACTIVE?

- ☐ A.
- ☐ B.
- ☐ C.
- ☐ D.

I am over 17.
Occupation ....
Nationality..
Your Sex (M/F) ....
Your Waistline .... Your Age..................
Height of person you wish to meet
Min .... Max............................
Surname ....
First Name ....
Address...
....
....

INTRODUCTION

Sir Norman Tonsil: A short time ago I saw fit to consult a doctor. Or rather I saw unfit, since I had become worried that it was some months since I had last seen my feet, and I was having difficulty getting my cigar over my stomach.

He gave me a complete examination, including asking me impertinently if I had moved my bowels that morning. I informed him that I had not and that he would find them round the back of my trousers as per usual.

Having taken my pulse, my temperature and my credit card he concluded that my measurements of 46-40-54 were somewhat too high... especially for a neck size. His advice was a diet and I reluctantly agreed. Unfortunately I was already committed to too many lunch engagements to go on a diet myself, so I decided to put my staff on a diet instead. The result has done me a power of good. Already most of them have lost several pounds while I have gained hundreds as a result of not having to pay for their lunches. In addition, I am delighted to say that I have got rid of my ulcer and given it instead to Martin Brown by threatening to terminate his contract.

Finally, my doctor suggested that as a service to the community I might like to carry a donor card around with me. I therefore now have this card on my person at all times.

> # KIDNEYS
> in white wine and mustard sauce
> # CARD

This means that in the event of my being knocked unconscious people will always know what to cook for me when I come round.

Anna's Diet Diary

Anna Daptor has been recommending on the Fit and Fat show that you keep a daily diary in which you put down honestly what you have consumed and can therefore tell if you're keeping to your diet.

Here is an extract from Anna's diary for Sunday November 9th.

9th SUNDAY

24th after Trinity
Remembrance Sunday
Cats go out

WEEK 45 (313–52)

9.0	½ Grapefruit. ½ Cup Black Coffee (De-caff)
12.0	½ oz Bran. Teaspoon Yoghurt.
12.15	A small gin + tonic (Slimline)
12.30	Piece wholemeal bread (no butter) 1oz Cottage cheese
12.35	A gin + tonic.
12.45	Two pieces wholemeal bread + butter.
1.05	A large gin + tonic
1.15	A sausage roll, Bacon egg, fried bread + ch
1.30	A pint of lager
Later	2 packets crisps Pork pie
	2 pints lager
Later still	PIZZA Treacle tart + cream
	4 pints bitter 3 lbs potatoes
	in cream + syrup
	½ Bottle Sweet Cooking Sherry
	6 Bowls Spaghetti in sugar sauce
	TOTAL CALS 125,000

SPECIAL KEEP FIT PULLOUT
(See The Fit and Fat Show, Thursday 11.) If you are unable to pull out these pages then you should follow all the advice we give you. At the end of reading the advice you should be motivated enough to pull out the pages and throw them violently away

ANNA'S FIT AND FAT

EXERCISE PROGRAMME

How Anna looks slim

Skipping exercise
Some of you might like to skip exercise completely but I find that just a little does help you build up a healthy appetite.

Exercise one Eating on the spot.

Exercise two The parallel bars. For this you simply need two bars of chocolate parallel to you at arms' length and you stretch out to them, hold that postition for a moment, then bring your arms back in towards your body and eat the bars of chocolate.

Anna lets you into one of her slimming secrets

BEFORE

AFTER

What's Anna's secret? Bigger clothes That's all there is to it.
   And you can still continue to eat as much as you like.

KEEP FIT WITH THE STARS

his week:

Lord Olivier plays golf

ext week: Oliver Reed plays snooker with a rge pink giraffe.

Darlings, the very first thing you should do is to address the ball. So…

Oh ball! Speed ye on your winged way; and may your passing carve a silver trail of zephyrs through the azure sky.

PILL BOX

ournalist and mother of hildren Jean Walker has ritten countless books on ealth and its relationship illness, and she swears y a diet of pills

I always carry a small box ith me everywhere I go, and asically it enables me to go rough the day without eating, rinking or going to the toilet. I I need to do is take one very four minutes.

The orange one's Vitamins A D, the pink one's Vitamin C, e brown one's an iron tablet o it's inedible, of course), the lue one's to keep my blood ressure down, and the beige ne's to bring it back up again ecause it's dangerous to let it et that low.

Then there's a tablet that elps me be lively and ener- etic, and a yellow one that elps me get through the run f the mill chores. The red ones elp me pick up the kids from chool at half past four, the urple ones help with the oovering and light dusting hursday mornings, and the reen one helps me wash the ar on Saturdays. That's a hampoo capsule, and I put it the end of a hose.

Then the large black one is an anti-depressant in case I receive any bad news during the day; the grey one's a sed- ative in case I receive too much good news during the day; and the postcard is just in case I don't receive any news during the day.

Finally, the white pill is an as- pirin, which I take to relieve the blinding headaches I get from taking so many pills.

Beat That Meat

Donald Dewhurst tells us how to stay 'Fighting Fit on Vegetarian Foods'.

Unfortunately, Mr Dewhurst was rather too weak to lift a pen and tell us himself how to stay 'Fighting Fit on Vegetarian Foods,' so instead Anna Daptor tells us about some of Donald's ideas.

Mr Dewhurst's basic belief is that you are what you eat and by the look of him he's been eating a lot of turnips recently. He also thinks it's important to know what the word 'vitamin' actually means. Apparently it comes from the Latin 'vita' meaning 'life', and 'mins', which apparently means mins. So the whole thing really means 'Life Mins'. I feel that with that knowledge I can die happy.

Finally, Mr Dewhurst's sug- gestion for the week is the Onion and Garlic diet. My advice is that, if you have any close friends who you wish to keep, ignore Mr Dewhurst and go on my Cream and Butter Diet instead.

Guide to Eating Out

It's always a problem losing weight if your job involves a lot of entertaining. So for all advertising executives, T.V. producers and rest- aurant guide compilers, here's the Radio Active Guide to Eating Out.

As an aperitif

DO: Order a tonic water, Perrier or slimline fruit juice.

DON'T: Order a pint of cream sherry and a Guinness chaser.

During your meal

DO: Eat your food slowly, allowing time for your stomach to digest it.

DON'T: Cram as much food as possible in your mouth so that you are unable to breathe or see out.

When you have finished

DO: Push anything you can't eat to one side and place your napkin on the table.

DON'T: Smother your nap- kin in salad cream and try to eat it.

After the meal if you feel slightly bloated

DO: Gently loosen your belt one or two notches.

DON'T: Drop you trousers round your ankles and rest your paunch on the table.

And finally, if you are with someone who has a weight problem

DO: Avoid drawing attention to their size.

DON'T: Prod their stomach and shout loudly, 'You don't sweat much for a fat girl.'

Anna Daptor dips into her shopping basket and comes up with this week's Super Savers!

BROOKE BOND TEA-BAGS
80 tea-bags, a bargain at just 94p from Fine Fare.

HEINZ BAKED BEANS
just 24p for an 8oz. can at Tesco's.

RADIO ACTIVE'S SUPERSAVER BARGAIN OF THE WEEK

KING-SIZE VIBRATOR
just 95p for a really good 10 inches from Thrilloid Products. An absolute bargain, I can assure you.

ADVERTISEMENT, BUT WE'RE PUTTING IT IN VERY SMALL LETTERS AT THE TOP OF THE PAGE, SO HOPEFULLY YOU'LL THINK IT'S REALLY ONE OF THE FEATURE ARTICLES.

52

Introducing a brand new concept in diet books

How to lose weight painlessly

JEAN WALKER

How to lose weight with a bit of pain

JEAN WALKER

Journalist and mother of children, Jean Walker's guide to losing weight takes you right through from the easy stages of calorie-counting and regulating your fat intake to some of the dramatically effective methods of weight loss developed by Torquemada and some of the more extreme members of the Spanish Inquisition. They include a fully illustrated set of low-calorie recipes, and a complete glossary of sado-masochistic equipment for the everyday domestic kitchen. These three volumes follow on from Jean Walker's best forgotten **Lose Weight by Losing the Will to Live: a Strict Diet for People Who Have Been Very Naughty**

How to lose weight with quite a lot of pain and possible loss of life

JEAN WALKER

This 3 book set just 50p each plus P & P*

Your money back if you are not satisfied or dead

* Pounds & Pounds

20 Things You Never Knew About Jesus Christ

Jesus Christ must be one of the most popular figures around! Popular with young and old alike! But do you know all there is to know about him? Here are twenty fascinating facts about our Redeemer!

Philip 'Nutter' Fanshaw

1. Jesus was born around 0 B.C. which by an amazing coincidence stood for Before Christ.
2. As a child Jesus was often picked on and bullied, but found he was able to find favour with other children by performing miracles in the playground.
3. Jesus would have preferred to have been an architect, but failed the exams, and was therefore forced into becoming the Lord Our Saviour who died for our sins.
4. Contrary to common belief, Jesus never actually visited the Holy Land.
5. Jesus Christ's real name was Philip Arthur Fanshaw and He was brought up in Dagenham, Essex.
6. At the age of 25, He gave up performing miracles and redeeming mankind to become a second-hand car dealer, specialising in Volkswagen campers.
7. Jesus' parents, contrary to biblical dogma, were Cyril and Vera Fanshaw and were both Welsh, moving to Essex with Cyril's work for United Biscuits.
8. Jesus' hobbies, again passing almost without mention in the Bible, were in fact drinking lager, playing darts and going to discos with friends.
9. Jesus spent most of His time, not with His disciples as is widely believed, but with His long-standing girlfriend, Sharon, who worked for Sketchley's, the dry-cleaning people.
10. Far from being a prolific performer of miracles, Jesus (or Phil as he was known to his close friends) could only do one trick well – that of flicking a beer mat up off a table and catching it with the same hand.
11. Somewhat unexpectedly, He was not a great fan of gospel music or hymns, preferring to listen to U2 or Simple Minds on His Escort stereo.
12. Jesus owned no donkeys or mules. His only pet was a budgerigar called Prince, and being near to donkeys or horses gave him hay-fever, for which he took pills.
13. Jesus Christ was a football fan. He supported Ipswich, being the nearest First Division side, and played on Sundays for the Old Stag Rovers.
14. Known to His teammates as 'Nutter', Jesus was a centre-forward, good in the air but lacking the close ball control to be deadly around the box.
15. Far from being crucified in Jerusalem at the age of 33, Christ settled down with a filing clerk called Paula, whom he married in Basildon at the age of 29.
16. Paula Christ is the daughter of both her parents.
17. Their two daughters Mandy and Trixy have not yet been born.
18. In 1947 Jack Kramer won Wimbledon.
19. I can't stand Su Pollard.
20. Mark Phillip's penis is apparently 8 inches long.
21. The researchers on this feature have been fired.

A Word from God

terest and conviviality and play, and jests and joking and banter and tomfoolery, and humour and wit and whimsicality and drollery.

But that's not all there is to it. Because it's also about beauty and splendour and magnificence and brilliance; about sublimity and grandeur and nobility and radiance, and fairness and loveliness and grace and perfection; about delicacy and refinement and majesty and wonder, and conviction and belief and promise and expectation and belief, and courage and heroism and fearlessness and valiance. And I don't think we should forget that. ■

THOUGHT FOR THE DAY

'Frankly, my dear, I don't give a damn!'

We look forward to a new series of 'Radio Film Night' which includes, amongst other things, a first for radio: the transmission of several major feature films in their entirety

British cinema: Isle of Dogs

Radio Film Night
Thursday 11.0

OF COURSE, few occasions can be more important for a British radio station that prides itself on its concern about local issues than a Film Festival in the South of France. **Mike Flex** went to Nice for a month for the two-week film festival.

'Undoubtedly this year's Nice Film Festival was the premier festival of its kind in the town this year. The big question was: who would win the coveted Prize D'Oor?

'In fact the winner was Andrzej Wajda, the Polish director, who scored a notable hit with a follow-up to his films *Man of Iron* and *Man of Marble* called *Man About the House*, starring Richard O'Sullivan as a disillusioned steel worker in Gdansk.

'The German entry, and winner of the Prize D'Oormat, was a nine and a half hour epic based on a short story by Thomas Mann. I only regret that I was unable to see the film myself owing to a pressing beach party. Entitled *Die Grosse Fahrte* it told the story of the Second World War from a different viewpoint. The Americans come in on the German side, Germany wins, Britain is carved up between the Russians and the Allies, and 20 years later Germany beat England in the World Cup Final after extra time.

'The French entry was the sex comedy, *Une Affaire, Deux Affaires*, which tells the everyday story of a woman who suspects her husband of being unfaithful to her. Pursuing him one day she bumps into someone who appears to be her identical twin but turns out to be a male transvestite who is having an affair with her cat. Then the now-classic eternal triangle is formed when she bumps into an old lamp-post and falls head over heels in love with it, only to find that the lamp-post is married to the transvestite. A familiar recipe maybe, but one that certainly seemed to strike a chord with all the French audience down there, which to my mind only lends more weight to the argument that garlic really does affect the brain. Nevertheless it won the slightly coveted Prize Patio D'Oor.

'The winner of the not very coveted at all Prize Cat Flap was a four hour existentialist farce, *Gay Bulgaria*, in which a doctor from Sofia reconciles his fate with the oneness of his cosmic self, whilst his mother-in-law maintains that the inner being is independent of extraneous universal imperatives – with hilarious consequences.

'Outside the competition Australian cinema was represented by the film *I'm Just Going Outback for a Minute*, which, like many of their recent films, featured lots of beautiful scenery marred only by lots of rather bad Australian actors standing in front of it. And Oivind Vinstra was particularly interested in the short season of Norwegian films, which appeared to conform to the age-old story line of lusty young farmers and their love for various items of agricultural equipment.

'Steven Spielberg's latest picture was eagerly awaited, and although it was not quite finished in time for the festival, an audience of dinner-jacketed celebrities happily queued for three hours outside the chemist's waiting for the film to be developed.'

MEANWHILE **Mike Channel** investigated the state of the British cinema. 'While the rest of the Radio Active team were off sunning themselves in Nice I was detailed to produce a report on the state of the British cinema, and let me tell you that few cinemas can be in a worse state than the one I was sent to – the Gaumont Empire on the Isle of Dogs. They were showing a short season of Hitchcock, most appropriately in fact, because my visit was a series of hitches and cock ups.

'Since there were no lights or signs to guide me, I found myself in a cupboard, a toilet, a projection box and back out in the street again before finally stumbling into the actual auditorium where I was greeted by an usherette reading a book. Consequently instead of tearing my ticket she tried to tear off the top of my finger.

'She was most insistent that I took my allocated seat and I was therefore somewhat surprised when the lights came up to discover that there were only two other people in the cinema. One of them was seven foot tall and sitting directly in front of me, and the other one was sitting directly behind me with his feet on my shoulders.

'The lights went down and an expectant hush came over the cinema as a picture of a burning cigarette appeared on the screen and went in and out of focus for a few minutes. During this time a voice informed us that this had been designated a No Smoking cinema, and for the convenience of those people who wished to smoke there was a cubicle in the conveniences.

We were reminded not to leave our bags on the floor unattended since their staff were very poorly paid and most had criminal records.

'The curtains then closed again so that they could reduce the size of the screen for the actual film, and during the 25 minute gap I approached the usherette about the possibility of buying a choc ice and was immediately evicted from the cinema.' ■

DURING the series **Oivind** will be giving various interviews with top movie stars, several of which will actually be in English. He kicks off by talking to Harrison Ford.

Oivind: So Harrison Ford, what do you think you are doing at the moment?
Harrison Ford: What am I doing at the moment?
Oivind: Ya.
Harrison: Well, I'm here to publicise *Drawl*, the new John Huston movie.
Oivind: What good is it?
Harrison: How good is it?
Oivind: Ya. Of course.
Harrison: Very good I'd say, but then I'm in it.
Oivind: Ya. Not many people like you as an actor.
Harrison: Pardon me?
Oivind: There are not many people like you as an actor.
Harrison: Oh! Right. Thank you.
Oivind: So how big are your parts?
Harrison: What?
Oivind: So how big are your parts?
Harrison: My part in the film? How big is it?
Oivind: Ya.
Harrison: I play the leading role of Ed who murders his sister played by Sissy Spacek.
Oivind: Did you get it on with her?
Harrison: Yes, we got on very well together.
Oivind: I believe she is a real prostitute.
Harrison: Pardon me?
Oivind: A real prostitute to work with.
Harrison: A professional.
Oivind: Ya.
Harrison: Yeah, she's very good at her work.
Oivind: So, what's happening now?
Harrison: With my career you mean?
Oivind: Ya.
Harrison: Ah well, I'm currently working on a political thriller directed by Nicholas Roeg.

Harrison Ford & Oivind Vinstra

Oivind: What's the point of that?
Harrison: The point of the film?
Oivind: Ya, of course.
Harrison: Well, it's about the way in which information is suppressed by the American government.
Oivind: Oh! Sexy!
Harrison: Not really, no. It comes out in about three weeks, anyway, and it's called *Info*.
Oivind: Better beware of that then.
Harrison: Better look out for it, yes.
Oivind: Good. Ya. Well, thank you for talking with me about these films of yours. And I hope you have more luck in the future.
Harrison: Yes, I couldn't agree more.
Oivind: And on with the music. ■

LATER in the series we'll be profiling the Bagel brothers, the two men who effectively took over control of the British film industry when they took over Canny Films.

See what Lizzie really meant by 'I shall make you shorter by a head.'
Execution of quite a different sort!

Anna Daptor's Joke Page

This week Anna shows you how to have fun with foreigners. Just choose half a dozen of your favourite jokes and translate them! Here are some of Anna's favourites for you to try out — and just see the reactions they get!

Doctor who? Voilà!

How does he smell? Ja!

ENGLISH

1. My dog's got no nose.

How does he smell?

Awful!

2. Excuse me, do you sell after-shave?

Certainly, sir. Walk this way.

If I could walk that way, I wouldn't need after-shave

3. Knock-knock!

Who's there?

Doctor.

Doctor who?

That's right!

4. Why do little bears walk softly?

Because they can't walk hardly.

5. Why does President Mitterand only have one egg for breakfast?

I don't know.

Because one egg's 'un oeuf.'

FRENCH

Mon chien n'a pas de nez.

Est-ce qu'il sent affreux?

Oui!

Est-ce que vous vendez l'après-rasage?

Oui, monsieur. Suivez-moi.

Si je pouvais te suivre, je n'aurais pas besoin de l'après-rasage!

Frappe-frappe!

Qui est la?

Monsieur le médecin.

Monsieur le médecin qui?

Voilà!

Pourquoi les petits ours marchent-ils doucement?

Parce qu'ils ont beaucoup de difficulté en marchant!

Pourquoi Chancelier Kohl n'a plus qu'un oeuf pour le petit déjeuner?

Je ne sais pas.

Parce qu'un oeuf est 'assez'.

GERMAN

Mein Hund hat keine Nase.

Stinkt er schrecklich?

Ja!

Entschuldigen Sie bitte! Verkaufen Sie Kölnische Wasser hier?

Jawohl, mein Herr. Kommen Sie mi

Wenn ich so laufen konnte, würde ich kein Kölnisches Wasser brauche.

Klopfe-klopfe!

Wer ist da?

Herr Doktor.

Herr Doktor wer?

Du hast recht!

Warum laufen kleine Bären leise?

Weil sie kaum laufen können!

Warum hat Frau Thatcher nur ein Ei fürs Frühstück?

Das weiss ich nicht.

Weil ein Ei 'genug' ist!

ODD LETTERS

Martin Brown: Mentally certifiable or just a little bats in the belfry?

AT FIRST I thought that Martin Brown was just a little slow on the uptake but having had the misfortune of hearing him again I realise that I was unfair; what we have here is almost certainly a case of certifiable mental derangement, a homage to catatonia, a man who is both round the bend and up the pole at the same time, someone with enough screws loose to bring down all the library shelves in the country, someone with a colony of bats in his belfry who have obviously been interbreeding for far too long, a stark staring potty cuckoo – in short a moron.

Dr Heinz Wooley
British Institute of Advanced Psychiatric Disorders

Martin Brown: more?

Moron?
Why do you employ Martin Brown? The man is a moron.
Brian Hope
The Malsters Arms

Personal hygiene
I must complain in the strongest possible etc. about a man called Martin Brown whom I heard performing a noisy and quite unnecessary act of personal hygiene during his programme last Thursday.
Archbishop of Canterbury
Canterbury, Kent

Violence
I would like to complain about violence on Radio Active. There is not enough of it, in particular not nearly enough towards Martin Brown.
Patrick McGrath
Marylebone Magistrates Ct., London W1

Martin Brown replies: *Thank you all very much for your views – all very well argued and fair. I have, however, asked the Radio Active Times to print a few of the many hundreds of fan letters I get every week.*

Martin Brown is very good.
Mr Brown Martins

Martin Brown? He is very good, I think.
Mr Martin Brownlow

Could we please have more of Martin Brown? I think he is very good.
Martin Brown (Mrs)

Shell Shocked
I was most offended to hear that you are planning to broadcast a show about D-Day. I died in two world wars for this country so I don't expect people to make fun of me and thousands like me.
Colonel 'Mitch' Mad
Home

● *Please note that in order to make your letters suitable for publication they may be shortened, re-written, have silly spelling mistakes inserted and generally buggered about with so you end up saying the complete opposite of what you intended.*

Dear God
Could you please tell me, what was the hymn broadcast by the Right Rev. Rev. Wright at the end of the show last Tuesday?
Mrs Eileen Gumm
Gwent

More Hymns
Could the Right Rev. Rev. Wright please play *Jerusalem* for my husband's birthday next Tuesday?
Mrs Colleen Bunbury
Banbury

Rough End of a Pineapple
The Right Rev. Rev. Wright. He wants the rough end of a pineapple up his backside.
Alan McNixon
Gorbals, Glasgow

The Right Rev. Rev. Wright writes: *(1) All Things Bright and Beautiful. (2) By all means. (3) I'm afraid this question seems to stray too much into the medical field for me to answer.*

Traffic service in sticky jam
I must express my dissatisfaction with your traffic reports ever since you bought your new high-powered helicopter. My journey to Swindon every morning is not helped in any way by reports of traffic jams outside Kingston, Jamaica.

Also, why are the reports now only broadcast fortnightly?
Christopher Tobin
Wilts.

The producer of our traffic reports will be replying in full to these criticisms just as soon as he gets back from Antigua.
– LETTERS EDITOR

General Whingeing
I was most upset by one of your 'Disc Jockeys' asking someone to 'look here'. Remarks like that are distressing to blind people since they also serve to remind them of their condition. Also by using the word 'here' you may well have offended your many thousands of deaf listeners.
Doris C. Pringle
Home Counties

Potty
I was most offended by your presenter suggesting I 'rush out and buy the latest record on the Radio Active label'. Thoughtless remarks like that are deeply upsetting to those of us who can't afford records.
Colin Crump
Newcastle

More Silly Old Codgers
I wish to complain very strongly about broadcasting your 'Bogie' Awards show from the Balmpot Hotel, Bournemouth.

Don't you realise that many people in Bournemouth lost their lives in the last war? How insensitive, then, to broadcast an awards ceremony of all things from there!
Mrs Stiles
Bradford, West Yorks

More Bogies
I found the awards given out at your annual Bogies to the cinema industry most offensive. Did it not occur to anyone that there are a great many films made about the war in which a lot of people died?
Charles Lowndes
The Falkland Islands

Requests
I'd like to take the opportunity of your letters page to Hi to Trevor, and I'd like to say I'm sorry Trevor, and hope you're still able to cycle. Good luck with the op and see you soon in court.
Deborah Mailer
Washington

Neighbourliness
I live just round the corner from the station and I would like to make a request. Please keep the noise down a bit or I will take immediate action.
Fanny Burnley
The red house on the corner

A ROOM OF MY OWN

Nigel Pry

ROVING reporter Nigel Pry describes his taste in interior decor as being 'literally, yes, my taste in decor for the inside'. His unique style of reporting, regarded by the charitable as gibberish, has taken Nigel to the far-flung corners of the world. Sadly for us all, he has always managed to find his way back. And with him he has brought a number of *objets d'art* which he chooses to parade in his toilet.

The wicker elephant which Nigel picked up on a mistaken trip he made to New Delhi when he was asked to report on *A Passage To India* he now uses as a toilet roll holder to remind him of the food he ate there, and the hospitals he stayed in.

The 'New York' T-shirt which adorns one of the walls he bought in New York Airport and keeps to remind him of what he was left wearing in the arrivals lounge after he had been strip-searched by officials looking for drugs.

The gaily coloured paisley-patterned tie Nigel bought in Bangkok, on another journey he made by mistake when he was asked to cover the London Marathon. He bought the tie because he was in Thailand, thinking this was a joke. His second mistake of the journey. It's now used to hang the air-freshener from the ceiling.

On his trip to Sydney, Australia, to cover the Siena Horse race, Nigel picked up another of his prize possessions, which has pride of place above the cistern – his boomerang, or as Nigel describes it, 'this strange bendy stick-thing which, yes, throwing it all round and round, literally a circle, and back in the hand. Ow!' Interestingly, Nigel now uses it as a toilet brush.

The former plant on top of the cistern is something Nigel brought back from Nigeria, after being asked to report on the Chelsea Flower Show. Its more than slightly dead appearance is evidently due to the harsh winter which it spent upside down in a dustbin. ∎

MARTIN BROWN'S TECHNICAL GLOSSARY

ACOUSTICS. Game played by racing bits of stick under a bridge.

AM. Technical term often used about yourself, e.g. I AM Martin Brown.

FM. F. Martin. Technical term often used about me, e.g. That F– Martin.

BOOM. As in microphone boom. Noise I make when I hit the microphone.

CANS. Things you wear on head during programme. Also metal containers for soup, beans, catfood etc. Also often worn on my head during programme.

CRETIN. Funny noise I seem to hear a lot down my cans (see Cans).

(Hope you like all the cross referencing, it took me nearly a week.)

RUMBLE. Noise made by my stomach during programme. Often cured by Feedback.

FEEDBACK. Technical term for someone coming up behind me during programme and feeding me, i.e. giving me food, e.g. a banana.

BASS FEEDBACK. Banana fed up bottom.

HISS. Noise from control box I get on my cans during my programme (also see Cretin).

HUM. Noise I make during my programme.

OHM. Another noise I make.

JACK PLUG. Name of the studio engineer, I think.

MIXER. Tonic water, bitter lemon, etc.

MIXING DESK. Studio control desk with lots of flashing lights over which I often spill tonic water, bitter lemon, etc.

TABLE AND CHAIR. Complicated technical arrangement in studio which enables me to speak into the microphone, unless I have mistakenly placed chair on top of table rather than by the side of it (see Last Tuesday).

MICROPHONE. Piece of broadcasting equipment most often used for stirring tea.

OMNI DIRECTIONAL MICROPHONE. Microphone I have just sent flying round the room, often while trying to shake tea off it.

TWEETER. Bird caught in speaker.

WOOFER. Dog caught in speaker.

WAVELENGTH. Length of time I get into my programme before I start waving for help. A short period.

WATT. Noise made by guests on my programme, often in response to questions such as, 'Who are you?'. Also noise made by me in response to sudden noise down headphone (see Hiss and Cretin). ∎

LISTENERS POLLS

Mike Channel and Mike Flex: how marvellous

BEST DJ *(Last year's positions in brackets)*

1. Mike Flex (2)
So, no surprises, eh? Ha ha. No, but seriously, I think I deserve it because I've been working pretty hard on my show all year. And let me say that in a very real sense this is an award for me and no one else, just in case any one was thinking that my success might be down to my producer or somebody. My only regret is that I had to knock my 'old chum' (and I mean 'old'), Mike Channel, off the top spot.

2. Anna Daptor (3)

3. Oivind Vinstra (–)
Ya ye har arbeide a Trondheim e Lillehammer, and on with the music.

4. Mike Hunt (4)

5. Nigel Pry (5)
(This includes all the spoilt ballot papers, which were taken as votes for Nigel).

6. Uncle Mike Stand (6)

7. Dick Barnes, The Weatherman (–)

8. The Pips of Big Ben (7)

8. Martin Brown (–)
What a great honour for me, in my first year as a Radio Active 'jock'. I didn't expect to be in the list at all, and of course a particular honour to be sharing the big number eight place with the pips of Big Ben, who I think provides some of the highlights of the day's broadcasting.

10. Mike Channel (1)
Well how marvellous, being voted best DJ last year was tremendous and being voted worst DJ this year is just as exciting, and if I was going to be knocked off my top spot by anyone then it's great to be beaten by someone with flair, taste and originality. It is,

however, a complete pisser to be beaten by a jumped up little turd like my 'friend' Flex. Looking down the list I also see that I have beaten by Uncle Mike Stand, who has been unable to broadcast all year on accont of being detained at Her Majesty's Pleasure, a man who doesn't speak an intelligible word of English (Oivind Vinstra), a man who doesn't speak an intelligible word of anything (Nigel Pry) and a man who isn't (Martin Brown). However, I see that there is some consolation for me in the other listeners' polls, where I am delighted to see that I have been voted Best Heating Appliance. ■

MARTIN BROWN'S CROSSWORD

Clues:

ACROSS

1. 8 pints make a...? (6)
5. Opposite of closed (3)
6. Opposite of knife and fork (5)
8. My favourite football team (5)
9. Fear of being in small spaces (only without the clau and raphobic bits) (2)
12. Big grey animals with long trunks that live in the zoo (9)
15. 'EZ' backwards (2)
16. The initials of someone called Ronald Ogilvy (2)
17. What you say if you can't hear someone (1)
18. The sound it makes when you go widgey-woos (6)

DOWN

1. Where I buy my vegetables (but not green!) (8)
2. People who live in the capital of Great Britain (8)
3. They lay eggs (3)
4. Opposite of moon (3)
7. What you say when you slip over (4)
10. 'STWT' backwards (4)
11. My first name (6)
13. My favourite vegetable (4)
14. What you do on the door if you want to be let in (3)
17. See 17 across (1)

Solution:

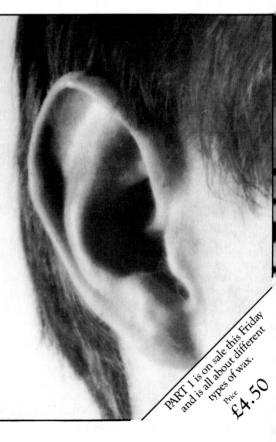

MIKE FLEX'S country mansion 'Dunjockin' is the location for Mike Channel's Sunday show next week. It covers some 5 acres of beautiful Berkshire countryside', Channel tells us, 'And what it covers it with is a hideous mock-tudor house, liberally decked out with fun-fur scatter cushions, and a number of pieces of furniture with Mike Flex's own initials on them — the "I" obviously has been painted out. At first glance, the house could be thought to belong to a colour-blind madman who has gone on a demented shopping-spree at Woolworths, and on closer inspection this appears to be largely true.' **Mike Channel on Mike Flex, Sunday 4am.**

Thursday sees the start of a new series which includes information about breast-feeding and the menopause, there'll be hints on flower-arranging and crochet work, and advice on pre-natal and post-natal problems. That's all on **It's a Man's World** with David Hughes at 11am.

Plus a NEW SEASON of programmes starting on Radio Active each morning:
So You Want to Make Something of It? Hints on things to make from waste products
Step Outside A series for ramblers
Take That A feature for amateur photographers
Teach You to Make Funny Remarks Some advice for budding comedy writers
And our religious affairs programme, **A Thundering Thwack in the Goolies.**

Mike Flex's Top Ten Teasers!

Each week Mike adds another prize for anyone who can get just ONE answer right! So far, if you can just answer one of the following correctly, you stand to WIN: a Radio Active yacht, a Radio Active Rolls-Royce, a Radio Active chateau in the Loire AND a Radio Active t-shirt! (Don't forget to tell us if you're small, medium or large.)

REGULAR listeners to Mike's programme – and odd listeners as well! – (that's one of Mike's favourite jokes – as regular listeners and odd listeners will know!) anyway, listeners to Mike's programme who tune in regularly will know that Mike's Top Ten Teaser competitions have become a household institution, ever since Mike took over from Mike Channel who moved to his new more popular slot of 4am on Sundays (that's another of Mike's favourite jokes!).

Here are Mike's Top Ten Teasers!

1. Who recorded *Led Zeppelin – Live At The Rainbow*?
2. According to the Commodores, *how many times a lady* was she?
3. Whose real name is Harry Webb?
4. Which is the top selling single, *White Christmas* or *Mull of Kintyre*?
5. Which country do the band *die Käfer* come from?
6. This is a trick question. True or false?
7. Which magazine is the most popular rock and pop magazine in the U.K.?
8. Where in the world would you find Copacabana?
9. Where does the name Bowie knife come from?
10. Tom Jones was famous as what in the 1960s?

For answers see p.61.

Answers to Mike Flex's Top Ten Teasers:
1. Vic Saunders, sound engineer at the Rainbow Theatre.
2. Six. "Once-twice-three times" which makes six in all. (1x2x3=6)
3. Mr Harold Webb, a toolfitter from Barnsley.
4. Neither. *Rivers of Babylon* outsold them both.
5. England, as *die Käfer* is German for the Beatles.
6. False. It's a perfectly ordinary question.
7. Which magazine is a consumer weekly that compares different brands of products.
8. In record shops, as it's a single by Barry Manilow.
9. From the word "knife" meaning a sharp instrument used for cutting things.
10. As a novel by Henry Fielding.

Station Identification

TED CHAPMAN of Fickle Bland Faye Chapman Wooley Coy Deft Lethal and Chalmers tells how they came to design the Radio Active logo.

'Designing the Radio Active logo was a real high-ticket account for us, and so I called a brainstorming meeting of our two top men: Steve "Softex – the toilet tissue that your finger doesn't go through" Kline, and Mike Redford, the man who came up with the concept of the artificial vagina in the milk chocolate commercial.

'After two hours of brainstorming Mike came straight to the point and said, "Who are the people who are going to buy this beer?"

'Well, we tossed that hot potato around for an hour or so until Steve made the crucial breakthrough: "Isn't this a radio station we're supposed to be advertising?". The clients loved the idea and then it was only a matter of three weeks' brainstorming at the Marrakech Hilton before we came up with the exciting design that elegantly combined all the complexities yet was eloquently simple in its simplicity.' ■

© Fickle Bland Faye Chapman Wooley Coy Deft Lethal and Chalmers

The Sir Norman Tonsil Lecture

This week the Radio Active Times reprints the entire Sir Norman Tonsil Memorial lecture, which takes its name from our distinguished founder and chairman and is delivered every year by a leading thinker and public figure (i.e. Sir Norman Tonsil)

IN this year's Sir Norman Tonsil lecture I have decided to start by focusing on one particular word and developing my theme from there. The word I have chosen today is 'procrastination'. As the Oxford English Dictionary defines it, the action or habit of putting off, the act of delay or dilatoriness. I intend to examine the nature of the procrastinator, the person who habitually delays and puts off attending to matters; who, in short, puts off until tomorrow what he should have done today.

I'm awfully sorry, that's as far as I've got.

The Sir Norman Tonsil Memorial Lecture will be broadcast in full from 10.00 to 11.30 on Thursday.

SNAP

North to play

North starts with the 3 of Clubs. East lays the Jack of Hearts. South lays the 2 of Diamonds. West now finds himself in a potentially winning position with an *ejusdem generis* 2 of Spades.

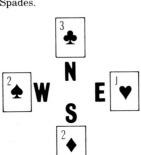

Ideal play would have been for West, on laying his card, to have established a pre-emptive proclamation of 'Snap', thus successfully forestalling South and sealing the game.

West's actual move was a hoarse exclamation of 'Oh shit! . . . Yes . . . Me . . . God, it's on the tip of my tongue! Bingo! . . . No . . . Check! . . . Oh, bugger!' accompanied by a vigorous flourish of the arms which caused a glass of red wine to be spilled over South.

South now had several choices of move. Firstly a defensive strategy, *videlicet*, a wet sponge accompanied by salt vigorously applied to the embryonic stain.

Secondly an attacking strategy, *viz.* a violent physical assault on West, accompanied by possible support from his partner, North.

In the event South opted for a combination – an attacking move with his East fist whilst North supported him in defence and sponged down his trousers.

The outcome, therefore, a ruled no contest and *da capo*.

Nappy Blot

New super absorbent Nappyblot keeps the wetness in and keeps your hands dry, _and_ you won't have to change the nappy for a month

THE ANNA RABIES COLUMN

Anna invites you to write in and get your personal, emotional or sexual problems off your chest and onto hers. Plus the chance to win £10 as our 'Letter of the Week' — the week's most embarrassing letter

LETTER OF THE WEEK

Dear Anna,
My husband is having an affair with another woman and every time I try to talk to him about it he starts threatening to leave me. I'm really at the end of my tether and I don't know what to do,
Yours,
Frantic of Chesham

Dear Frantic,
You must do the only thing you can do luvvie, and that's to go up to him and ask him quite openly if he's seeing another woman, and if he admits it then you'll have to face facts, luvvie. And my advice to you in that situation would be to kill him.
Anna

Dear Anna,
I've been married and living in Croydon for three years now, and for the past few months I've been having an affair with another woman. I'm sure you'll understand that given the circumstances I'd be grateful if you didn't publish my name.

Dear Peter Bainbridge,
No, I don't understand at all about not publishing your name.
I believe the only way you're going to solve your problem is to be completely honest with yourself. So Mrs Bainbridge, if you're reading this (or if anyone's reading this who knows her perhaps they'd let her know), your husband is having an affair with at least one other woman. Of course it could so easily be more.
Anna

Dear Anna,
My boyfriend wants to get engaged, but as I'm only fourteen my parents object. What should I do.
Yours,
Sandra

Dear Sandra,
Sleep with him, then marry him. Pre-marital sex is perfectly normal these days. And if your parents object because you're only fourteen then you'll have to kill them. In fact, on second thoughts sleep with them and then kill them. Pre-patricidal sex. Or kill them, then sleep with them. Necrophilia. Nothing wrong with it. You've got to come to terms with it sooner of later. We all have our lives to live and if that means having to murder Mummy and Daddy in cold blood then we just have to face reality. I know it's not easy, but then life never is.
Anna

Dear Anna,
My dog is rather ill but I'm reluctant to have him put down as I love him very deeply.
What should I do?
Yours, Katy

Dear Katy,
Sleep with it. One, you've got to come to terms with your sexuality some time. Two, you'll simply have to tell the dog that the relationship can't continue unless you get your oats. There's no need to feel ashamed about your abnormal sexual fantasies. I believe it can be very pleasurable for the dog too.
Anna

Introducing...

Naughty Bears

What makes Naughty Bears so unusual and irresistible to all but the most backwards of kiddies?

QUIET BEAR
He's at his happiest when he's got a firm grip on his pork sword and is giving it a vigorous rubbing

ACTION BEAR
He likes nothing better than to get out his massive throbbing punisher and give Looby Loo a good seeing to

It's probably their cute little cuddly bottoms, their realistically workable private parts and their penchant for getting into naughty positions with each other.

And of course each bear is made in washable fun fur to avoid possible embarrassment.

SMILEY BEAR
He wants it and he's going to get it

Simply fill in the Application form and your Naughty Bear will be sent to you straight away in a plain brown wrapper.

RESERVATION APPLICATION
Naughty Bears
P.O. Box 18. Teddington

Please accept my application for a *Naughty Bear*. I fully understand that if my Naughty Bear should be in any way damaged, split or interfered with it is my own responsibility. I am completely ready for my Naughty Bear.

Signature ....
Mr/Mrs/Miss/Teddy Bear............
Address ....
....

WOULD YOU MAKE A GOOD QUEEN?

ust fill in this carefully detailed uestionnaire and find out if you have hat it takes to become the next Queen f England.

. Most of my friends are:
- A. Dustmen
- B. Boxers
- C. Duchesses

2. I like to wear:
- A. Hats
- B. Handkerchiefs
- C. Crowns

3. When I meet a guy for the first time I usually say:
- A. Hello
- B. Hello Big Boy
- C. Arise, Sir

4. On my first date with a boy I:
- A. Let him hold my hand.
- B. Let him snog with me
- C. Let him snog with my personal security guard

5. At Christmas I like to:
- A. Put my feet up in front of the telly
- B. Carve the turkey
- C. Address the nation

6. I like opening:
- A. Presents
- B. Chocolates
- C. Parliament

7. I am used to treading on:
- A. Floorboards
- B Lino
- C. Corgis

8. I would like my son to be:
- A. A mini-cab driver
- B. A wholesale tobacconist
- C. King

ANSWERS:
Our Royal expert writes: If you scored lots of As then you stand a very good chance of becoming Queen in the not too distant future. If you scored Bs then you stand a jolly good chance of becoming Queen if we were ever to go over to a system of elected monarchy. If you scored exclusively Cs then the chances are you are an inmate of one of Her Majesty's more secure mental institutions OR you are already Queen, in which case I'm afraid you are not really eligible to enter this, Ma'am.

On this day

● On this day in 1894 inventor Charles Purdham was born. He invented a small black knob on the end of gas kettles which allows you to take the spout off without burning your fingers. He lived in poverty, died penniless and is remembered only by people compiling useless information.

● On this day in 1688 scientist Sir Isaac Newton's experience of sitting under an apple tree and having an apple fall on his head led him to invent the crash helmet.

● On this day in 1928 aviator William Donaghue flew single-handed from London to Dublin. The flight took 4 weeks, 5 days and 17 hours. The following year he did it in just 90 minutes by flying west.

● On this day in 1447 explorer Sir John Biddle discovered his wife making love to his best friend. Being a man of moderation and tolerance, he shot them both through the head, thereby inventing the handgun some 300 years before it was thought of.

● On this day in 1422 scientist Thomas Picton invented the Amstrad home computer, £399 plus VAT. Unfortunately no one had yet invented electricity, so he too died penniless.

● And finally, on this day in 2654 BC cave man UgUg invented language, when he dropped a large boulder on his foot. A fact documented by his wife, who, on hearing him cry out, shouted, 'Language!'

Kiddies' weekly news digest ...

COMPILED BY UNCLE MIKE STAND

HELLO KIDS. Well what a fun week it has been. First of all a government report out this week said alcoholism among kids has increased by over 30 per cent. Which is jolly good news for those of you who collect bottle tops.

WIN WAN the female panda arrived this week all the way from China to be mated with our very own Wang Wang. The two were introduced and crowds of laughing children applauded; Wang Wang broke out of the cage and killed ten of them before being destroyed.

On the international money markets the pound this week did this. Which means it's now worth only two packets of bubble gum and a bag of gobstoppers.

WELL WISHERS

RADIO ACTIVE has had some rather important and famous visitors since it went on air. Bailiffs, debt collectors, the fraud squad – the list is endless! But it's also had a fair number of showbiz stars. So take a look at some of the signatures we've collected – it's an all-star line up!

To all at Radio Active with love Sting

STING

To Radio Active, our favourite station. Lots of luck! Charles, Di and Harry

PRINCE CHARLES, PRINCESS DIANA AND PRINCE HARRY

Radio Active – that's my kinda station! Frank

FRANK SINATRA

To all my friends at Radio Active Lots of love Joan

JOAN COLLINS

God Bless Radio Active! Love and best wishes John Paul II

POPE JOHN PAUL